27 VIEWS OF DURHAM

BRAGTOWN

Ninth Street ←

Duke Chapel

Carolina Theatre

Durham County Public Library

TACOS

BURGER

SUNTRUST

→ East Durham

DURHAM BULLS ATHLETIC PARK

SunTrust Tower

PARRISH STREET

HAYTi HERITAGE CENTER

NCCU

27 VIEWS OF DURHAM

The Bull City in Prose & Poetry

Introduction by Steve Schewel

eno
publishers

27 Views of Durham: The Bull City in Prose & Poetry
Introduction by Steve Schewel
© Eno Publishers, 2012
All rights reserved

Each selection is the copyrighted property of its respective author
or publisher, if so noted on Permissions page, and appears in this volume
by arrangement with the individual writer or publisher.

Eno Publishers
P.O. Box 158
Hillsborough, North Carolina 27278
www.enopublishers.org

ISBN-13: 978-0-9832475-3-1
ISBN-10: 0-9832475-3-6
Library of Congress Control Number: 2012942157

Cover illustration by Daniel Wallace, Chapel Hill, North Carolina
Design and typesetting by Horse & Buggy Press, Durham, North Carolina
Distributed to the book trade by John F. Blair Publisher, 800.222.9796

Acknowledgments

A huge thank you to Steve Schewel and our twenty-eight writers who have created a literary montage of Durham, now and then.

Eno Publishers also wishes to thank Gita Schonfeld and Adrienne Fox for their careful editorial work on the views, and Daniel Wallace for his colorful rendering of Durham.

Eno Publishers appreciates the generous support the Mary Duke Biddle Foundation whose grant helped fund the publishing of *27 Views of Durham*.

Permissions

Some of the works in this volume have appeared in whole or in part in other publications.

Lewis Shiner's story, "Wonderland," originally appeared in *Black Clock* #8 (Fall 2007).

Ariel Dorfman's piece is adapted from his book, *Feeding on Dreams: Confessions of an Unrepentant Exile* (Houghton Mifflin Harcourt, 2011).

Barry Yeoman's essay, "The Morning After Amendment One," originally appeared on indyweek.com, the website of the *Independent Weekly* (9 May 2012).

Pam Spaulding's essay, "Boom," is adapted from her columns from the *Durham News* (19 May 2009 and 8 July 2009).

"The Sloping Hills," by Walter Matthew Brown, is excerpted from his memoir, *I Walked the Sloping Hills* (Stovepipe Publishing, 2010).

David Cecelski's "Shirley's Garden" originally appeared in the Raleigh *News & Observer* on 11 October 1998.

Chris Reid's "Gnawin' on Heaven's Door" is adapted from the blog, Carpe Durham, at carpedurham.com.

Jim Wise's essay, "A Sense of Place," is adapted from his book *Durham Tales* (History Press, 2008).

Table of Contents

VIEWS FROM BEFORE

VIEWS IN FICTION

STREET SCENES

HOMEWARD

DURHAM OUT LOUD

Preface

This book's title, 27 *Views of Durham*, is only a slight exaggeration—in fact, you'll find twenty-eight (instead of twenty-seven) perspectives of life in the much-storied Bull City. The views span neighborhoods, decades and generations, racial and cultural experiences, to create a sense of place.

Some of the views herein celebrate the city; others its grit. Some views expose its complicated past; others its still complicated present. Some shine a lens on a community evolving; some focus on the price of that change; others zero in on the imperative of change.

27 *Views of Durham* is not a guide in any traditional sense. It is more a literary montage: a composite created from a variety of genres—fiction, essays, poems, an oral history, even a Durham anthem. Our hope is that the book gives readers insight into life in Durham today and in the past, and into how twenty-eight of its inhabitants think about their home.

Elizabeth Woodman
Eno Publishers

Introduction

DURHAM'S GREATEST WRITER died last year having written precious little about Durham. Born in a small town in eastern North Carolina, Reynolds Price came to Duke as an undergraduate, earned a Rhodes Scholarship at Oxford, and returned to live, teach, and write for half a century. He wrote thirty-eight books in all—novels, memoirs, plays, essay collections, short stories, poems, children's books, theology, meditations on the writer's craft, and reflections on the spinal cancer that left him wheelchair-bound for the last years of his life.

Forty years ago, as a Duke sophomore from a small Southern town myself, I was lucky enough to take a class on John Milton from Mr. Price. Just to hear him read from *Paradise Lost* in his deep, resonant voice was reason enough to be there. I remember my dismay when he wrote "too flowery" in the margin of one of my essays. Otherwise, I hid in the back of the class, squeezed out a "B," and worshipped him silently from afar.

So imagine my happy surprise over the years when he acknowledged me, spoke to me with interest, and recommended me for graduate school and even the Rhodes (I didn't come close), or when he hailed me loudly across campus or outside the Regulator Bookshop from his wheelchair. Mr. Price insisted I call him "Reynolds," but I never did. As a Southern boy raised to respect my elder and betters, I never could.

Everyone in Durham who read fiction knew Reynolds Price was here in our midst, a great writer and a good man. It seems fitting to introduce this collection, *27 Views of Durham*, by remembering him, though ironically he wrote little about his adopted hometown. Mr. Price set his best novels, *Kate Vaiden* and the Rosacoke Mustian cycle, in the eastern North Carolina of his childhood and still others in England and Eden and Greensboro and Galilee.

Mr. Price is hardly alone in this literary neglect of our city. With notable exceptions such as Lewis Shiner, Carl Kenney, and Katy Munger, few writers have published fiction set in Durham. Ernest Seeman is also among those exceptions, and it took him thirty-seven years to complete his novel.

Seeman wrote what could be called the definitive twentieth-century Durham story. Born and raised in Durham, Seeman became head of Duke University Press in the 1920s and was known for his radical views and sympathy for labor. That worked out well for him until the great General Strike of 1934, the largest labor action in American history, swept the South. Hundreds of thousands of textile workers walked the picket lines from Alabama to Virginia on behalf of restored wages, better working conditions, and the forty-hour workweek. In Durham, more than 7,000 textile workers went out on strike, pouring from factories like Golden Belt and Erwin Mills and parading down Main Street.

At Duke, a group of students lit bonfires to support the strikers and wrote a satire lampooning the factory owners and their allies at the university. When Ernest Seeman came to the students' defense, the university administration gave him the sack.

So Seeman left town and eventually landed in a cabin in Tennessee where he began work on his Durham novel. At age ninety-one, he finally handed his 700-page manuscript over to his editor, who chopped it in half and got it published as *American Gold*, its name evoking brightleaf tobacco and the fortunes it spawned.

The truth is that *American Gold* isn't so much a novel as a series of vignettes, vivid portraits of poor country folks, black and white, and exotic outsiders, lured in and chewed up by the tobacco and textile machines of Durham in its Gilded Age.

At the end of the book, greed and the tobacco factories' "enchanted machines" themselves triumph over human decency. Still, Seeman's auto-biographical hero can't help himself—"his love for his home town was as futile as the blind unreasoning attachment of parents for a mindless and degenerate child."

Like Ernest Seeman, many writers today see Durham from the bottom up, and they can't help themselves either. They love this place. Essayist Pierce Freelon writes in this volume about returning to his native Durham with his young family, "I earned the dual privilege of being both a Durham explorer and ambassador."

Durham isn't quiet. The city that Seeman described as "gibbering, sobbing, crooning, shrieking, rattling" is still and always with us. It doesn't give a moment's peace. This can be taken quite literally. Just read Pam Spaulding's vignettes in "Boom"—the thud of the wrecking ball, tearing down one mall to put up another, and the crash of box trucks that regularly fail to clear the top of the downtown train trestle. Maybe the noise explains why there are more novelists living right now in one quiet, bucolic square mile of nearby Hillsborough than Durham has produced in its history.

While few have captured Durham in fiction, our city attracts more than its share of journalists and bloggers, essayists and advocates, historians and slam poets. They embrace the clang and clamor. They want to argue, to proclaim, to laugh out loud, to write late into the night, slouching blear-eyed toward their word-counts and deadlines.

True, the sweet rum smell of toasting tobacco no longer hangs in the air downtown, as it did for more than a century. The factory machines aren't clanging anymore. Now our writers take their arguments to Durham's new farm-to-table restaurants. They have their pick of fair-trade coffee shops when they look to settle in someplace with their laptops. They harangue each other at a food truck rodeo or over a local craft brew.

Last year *Bon Appétit* called Durham America's "foodiest" small town, and the *Daily Beast* named it the "most tolerant" city in the nation. Both *Black Enterprise* and *Money Magazine* listed it as the number one place to retire in America. Recently *Forbes* said Durham was the best mid-sized city for jobs, and *Businessweek* cited Durham as the third best city in America to ride out the recession.

Notwithstanding the surprising emergence of Durham as a cool place to live, our writers know that just over the centerfield fence at the gorgeous Durham Bulls Athletic Park, right next to the striking and popular Durham Performing Arts Center, loom the spanking new courthouse and the massive phalanx of the jail, as Dawn Baumgartner Vaughan writes in the opening of her essay, "Durham, Unvarnished."

Juxtaposed with the cool is the persistent reality, present and past, of poverty and discrimination. Here is one measure that isn't advertised by the Chamber of Commerce: Urban futurist Richard Florida recently ranked cities according to their wage inequality, and Durham came in fifth in the nation. White flight is resegregating Durham's public schools. One quarter of Durham's children live in poverty. Neighborhoods east and south of downtown are filled with boarded-up houses and vacant lots.

Like Ernest Seeman before them, our writers love their city but refuse to flinch from its reality. Among the 27 *Views*, Carl Kenney's story is most emblematic of Durham's double nature. He writes of a cozy coffee shop on a cold winter's day, a prosperous but stricken community waiting anxiously for a friend—a homeless man—to come in from the streets alive.

Jim Wise writes in these pages of Durham's repetitive history of sheer foolishness and the failed attempts to break that pattern. But he isn't disheartened by the failures. Rather he defends the effort. "In Durham," he writes, "civic life is a participant sport and everybody's eligible to play. And welcome too."

The folks who make up "everybody" in Durham are changing all the time. In *American Gold*, when the tobacco magnates need laborers with "clever hands" to roll cigarettes, they bring "a big cargo of Jew hands— Russkies . . . little gnomish chattery women with their funny boots and soutached garments . . . who could lick the brown cigarette papers" faster than anybody. The influx of Jews strikes fear in those concerned about the "twin pillars of world stability—southern womanhood and white suprem-acy." Seeman writes that to the town's "pure and sacred Anglo-Saxon soil came the Jew's fears, the Jew's wit and wisdom. To the sordid social silt of East Stogie Street arrived the Yiddish newspapers, the battered old silk hats and long greasy beards, and wild unworldly eyes of the rabbis. . . . The ring-ing singings of the Jewish anthem and the fervent Asiatic chantings and wailings." Then come the "the smart set" cracking "kike jokes" and the "age-old Shylock slanders and sucking-the-blood-of-Gentile-babies vilifications."

I came to Duke as an undergraduate in 1969 under what I now know to have been a "Jewish quota." But today Durham has a large, growing, and well-educated Jewish community, two vibrant congregations, and a sleek new Jewish Community Center. Durham's Jews live in a city that longtime Mayor Bill Bell likes to describe with pride as a "city without a majority." That is, with the influx of Hispanic and Asian residents, neither Durham's white nor black citizens make up a majority of the population.

While Durham's Jewish community may be prospering far from East Stogie Street, another group of immigrant laborers has followed them to Durham a hundred years later. These are the immigrants from Latin Amer-ica, many of them undocumented, who have traveled to Durham fleeing poverty in their own country in pursuit of a better life, such as the family Rodrigo Dorfman writes about in his essay, "El Nuevo South."

One quarter of the kindergartners in Durham Public Schools now speak Spanish as their first language, and in some schools that number is as high as 50 percent. These children and their families are learning to make their way in a difficult new world. The adults may be working atop the scaffold-ing, putting the finishing touches on the brand new courthouse, or working in the kitchens of the fabulous downtown restaurants. Most do not yet partake of the "participant sport" of Durham's civic life—but that time is coming.

It has already come for the most internationally acclaimed writer living in Durham, Ariel Dorfman—playwright, poet, memoirist, and novelist, as celebrated for his human rights activism as for his writing.

The descendant of European Jewish immigrants to South America, Dorfman as a young man worked in the administration of Chile's socialist president, Salvador Allende. When Chilean generals backed by the CIA overthrew the Allende government, Dorfman was forced into exile, and since 1985 he has been a professor at Duke. His themes are tyranny, torture, exile — and how to fight against them.

Like other recent Hispanic immigrants to Durham, Ariel Dorfman had to navigate the world in two languages. For him, Durham is "the place where my English and Spanish cease to war with each other." Like other writers in these pages, he argues, cajoles, confronts, wrangles, runs toward the action on the street and not away from it — a quintessentially Durham trait. Here is how Dorfman describes Durham in a phrase: "Home at last."

While Dorfman had to flee his home to find a new one in Durham, another distinguished writer and activist, Pauli Murray (1910–1985), had to flee Durham to find her voice and her future. As a young African American girl growing up in the West End, she felt the bitter sting of racism visited daily upon her capable, educated family. Determined to fight back, she graduated from Hillside High School in 1926 and left for New York to attend Hunter College. In 1938, she applied to law school at the University of North Carolina with the support of the NAACP, but was turned down because of her race. She went on to graduate from law school at Howard, the only woman in her class and the only graduate to receive a prestigious fellowship to Harvard — only to be rejected by that university, this time because of her gender. She became a cofounder of the Congress of Racial Equality (CORE), a friend and colleague of Eleanor Roosevelt and Thurgood Marshall, and a leading legal scholar for the civil rights movement. An early feminist, in 1977, at the age of sixty-seven, she became the first African American woman ordained as a priest in the Episcopal church.

It is in her 1956 memoir, *Proud Shoes: The Story of an American Family*, that this remarkable woman comes to terms with her Durham childhood. The book turns on the death of her grandfather, the family patriarch, in 1919.

22

Young Pauli's response to this event serves as a Durham writer's reminder of the ever-present hard truths beneath our city's prosperous new cool— and a reminder, too, that in Durham people have always fought back.

Murray's grandfather was buried in the family plot behind their home, separated only by an iron fence from the white Maplewood Cemetery where many of the dead were Confederate soldiers. Murray writes that "every Memorial Day or Decoration Day, the cemetery hillside was dotted with cross-barred Confederate flags. As a Union veteran, Grandfather was entitled to a United States flag for his grave, so every May I walked proudly through a field of Confederate flags hugging my gold-pointed replica of Old Glory . . . and planted it at the head of Grandfather's grave." She continues:

> This solitary American flag just outside the iron fence which separated it from the Confederate banners waving on the other side was an act of hunger and defiance. . . . It bore mute testimony to the irrefutable fact that I was an American and it helped to negate in my mind the signs and symbols of inferiority and apartness. . . . It was only a few feet from the main highway between Durham and Chapel Hill. I wanted the white people who drove by to be sure to see this banner and me standing by it. Whatever else they denied me, they could not take from me this right and the undiminished stature it gave me. For there at least at Grandfather's grave with the American flag in my hands, I could stand very tall and in proud shoes.

On November 20, 2011, Pauli Murray's one hundred and first birthday, Mayor Bell proclaimed Pauli Murray Day in Durham, and the community unveiled a state historical marker near the spot where she stood as a child in her proud shoes. The marker memorializes the achievements of one of Durham's most accomplished daughters, an exceptional activist on the national stage and a writer who reveals a harsh, critical chapter in Durham's past.

The inequalities of race and gender that Pauli Murray faced down are still with us, if diminished by the ongoing struggles of the civil rights and women's movements. In 2012, Durhamites faced down another inequality—the vote on Amendment One which proposed a state constitutional ban on the marriage of same-sex couples. While more than 60 percent of North Carolina voters approved it, the amendment suffered a crushing defeat in Durham where seven in ten voters opposed it, a margin of nearly 30,000 voters. As journalist Barry Yeoman, a gay man, writes in these pages, living in Durham during the Amendment One battle was "the redemptive aspect of this struggle," a redemption that Pauli Murray surely would have appreciated.

Yeoman writes of Durham, "I have never seen a community mount such a forceful, unified, creative response to a collective threat. I have never had so many neighbors tell me, 'Your battle is mine too.' The results of that Tuesday's election might solidify the sense of otherness with which I view my state and country. But my patriotism to my city has never been stronger."

Welcome to 27 *Views of Durham*. In these pages you'll find plenty of people standing tall in proud shoes.

Steve Schewel
Spring 2012

STEVE SCHEWEL is cofounder and president of the award-winning *Independent Weekly*. He is a writer and visiting assistant professor at the Sanford School of Public Policy at Duke University. He is a member of the Durham City Council and past member of the Durham board of education. A longtime youth soccer coach, he is an avid runner and reader, and fancies himself a pretty good cook.

Durham Grit

A Sense of Place

JIM WISE

OUR FIFTEEN-YEAR-OLD HAD JUST COME HOME after two weeks at camp in the mountains, and her eye happened to fall upon that morning's paper.

— They're *still* arguing about that stupid flag?!!

And who says Generation Y doesn't attend to current events?

Fatherly pride aside, yes, it was 1998 and they were still arguing about that flag — *they* being the Durham City Council and *that flag* a 600-square-foot Star-Spangled Banner that, flying high above a restaurant from a seventy-foot pole, got ticketed for two counts of flaunting the new sign ordinance.

This had been going on almost a year. They were *still* arguing. The argument showed no sign of ending, and, indeed, it would go on to unintended consequences, not so much for flags as for the city council. And therein lies an illustrative tale about our bully, gritty, and quirky hometown where tolerance (we're willing to put up with a lot) is prized but, still, has its limits.

What was going on was this:

In July 1997, city authorities told the restaurant manager his flag was ten times bigger and thirty feet higher than what the law allowed. When he refused to become law-abiding, he got a $25 fine and complained to a council member, who complained to a committee, which concluded it would not change the ordinance just to accommodate Old Glory, and in no time at all the city's sleuths had cited three more flag-waving institutions. Veterans and other folk as well were becoming upset.

At this point, the rest of the city council members chimed in. There were thirteen of them, so there was a great deal of chiming to do, and it took some time to let every voice be heard, which is very important in Durham sometimes, like when an election is coming up, which is every year for something or another. Two months after the issue came to light, with flags furled, the council voted to leave the law as it was.

The sign ordinance had been enacted nine years earlier to keep Durham beautiful, but many citizens felt that a law meant to curb billboards had no business with the American flag. The council's thorough debate and eventual vote had kept the sign ordinance in the public mind and the letters-to-the-editor columns, where it remained through the fall election as candidates of all persuasions covered their rhetorical chests, not to mention their rear ends, with affirmations of their deep-felt patriotism.

While that was going on, another diligent civil servant spotted another sort of sign scofflaw: a plastic cow that had, since 1963, stood atop a suburban convenience store on Chapel Hill Road. The store was best known, of course, as the "Cow Store." It seemed that the ordinance outlawed signs on top of places of business, but those already standing when the law took effect got a ten-year reprieve that was just about to run out. Looking ahead, city planners had some interns out taking names and pictures of noncompliants soon to be.

With Save the Cow a ringing refrain, the city council duly took the cow under consideration along with the flag and carried both into the new year. In February, the city created a subcommittee to talk about the sign ordinance. In May, with one rogue councilman's encouragement, the restaurant where the flag flap began defied the law and raised its banner again. The restaurant was fined $200 and the manager lowered the flag again. A month later, the subcommittee that the council formed recommended an ordinance amendment to exempt the U.S. flag. The council voted against it.

The council did, however, approve an amendment that let the plastic cow remain in place as a local historic landmark. The owner, however, was notified that his sign beside the street was three feet too high.

On Flag Day, June 14, the restaurant broke the law again and was fined $300. Then the Veterans of Foreign Wars, American Legion, Military Order of the Purple Heart, and Marine Corps League told City Hall they were going to raise an illegal flag of their own as a symbol of solidarity (the ordinance didn't say anything about solidarity) at the American Legion Post, and if the city did anything about it they would sue for a violation of the First Amendment.

Undaunted, the city wrote the American Legion a ticket; the Legion made a federal case of it. Then an alert citizen discovered that the flagpole atop the city's tallest building and most of those on public school grounds were too big, too.

So was the one at City Hall itself.

This was about the time our fifteen-year-old got home from camp.

A year after the whole mess had begun, the city council finally got the message and let flags fly up to 260 square feet and flagpoles stand up to seventy. But while public attention had been riveted on the flag flap and cow controversy, the city council had voted itself a 37 percent pay raise, and once the public caught on, it got upset about that, too. Perhaps with visions of torch- and pitchfork-bearing peasants dancing in their heads, the City Hall Thirteen reduced their raise to nine percent, but it was too little and too late. The elected leadership had dithered over flags and cows while dope was dealt, potholes proliferated, and Raleigh Realtors recited the latest reasons why clients new to the area would never want to live in Durham.

Understand, this was not the first act of theatrical absurdity to which the city had treated taxpayers in recent memory. There had been loans to nonexistent small businesses; an investment in high-tech garbage trucks that proved an expensive lesson in the-more-you-add-on-the-more-there-is-to-go-wrong; an interminable indecision on what to do when the city dump ran out of room; a consultant paid to assess whether city employees were sufficiently sensitive—all just went to show that any time Durham put its official best foot forward there was plenty of ammunition to shoot it with and somebody was locked and loaded.

Before the sign ordinance was even written, one local worthy pointed out that Durham had a big, tall water tower in full view of the freeway coming into town from the airport, and figured there ought to be some expression of civic pride up there to let incomers know just where they were.

But of course! said the booster set, so the City Hall Thirteen took up the cause. They talked and thought and thought and talked some more, week after week.

What should Durham have to say? "Welcome to Durham"? "Welcome to Durham, North Carolina"? "Enter at Your Own Risk"?

And what about the color scheme? Should it be Duke blue on white, white on Duke blue, North Carolina Central University maroon on gray, or vice versa? Durham Bulls orange and blue? All-American red, white, and blue? After due diligence, the municipal parents opted for "Welcome to Durham" in blue, using the New Gothic Bold type style, but then some Bull citizens objected that there was no mention of "City of Medicine," the then-current slogan for building civic self-esteem. At that point one council member said the whole idea was "mindless boosterism"; and another said, "Welcome to Mayberry"; and a third suggested that further research was called for. The council took another vote and agreed to forget about it.

Eleven years later, the water tower—by then embarrassingly rusty—finally got a new coat of paint. Plain, utilitarian white. First, however, the tank's surface had to be sanded smooth, and to keep from making a mess

32

the whole water tower was covered with a great big sheet of plastic. So for months the water tower became a tall, round-topped structure encased in sheer plastic. It stood erect beside the highway, proclaiming something to the passing throngs best left to the imagination.

But the point of all this is, when someone in Durham says she's mad as hell and not going to take it any more, you might want to look out. Our town may be tolerant but, as said above, there are limits and in 1998 they had been reached. The flag, the cow, the raise, combined with long-festering inanities, galvanized the hoi polloi to whack the city council down to size. From thirteen members to seven, to be specific, on the assumption that six fewer voices to be heard would, if nothing else, get council meetings over with quicker than had been the custom. Council members advised caution, if not further research, and claimed it would be a lot of bother to put the proposition out for a vote in time for the November election day. And did the taxpayers really want to pay for a special election, over nothing more than seven seats at City Hall?

Yes.

In a special December referendum the voters voted, and the city council went through a crash diet; and so it remains, thinner if not necessarily in fighting trim to this very day. A federal appeals court eventually dismissed the American Legion lawsuit over flag flying, affirming a municipality's right to rule that size matters, but the cow stands historically tall atop the convenience store—later turned into a taqueria.

Yes, that summer day, they were still talking about the flag.

Yes, our town can resemble a loony bin where the loons are running things.

It hasn't been just the city council. School board meetings were for a time so nasty you'd have thought Jerry Springer was the chairman, and their cable broadcasts became local teenagers' must-see TV. The county commissioners fired the county manager, then turned around and hired him right back after the next election. And so it goes. Civic leaders get so worked up over drugs and gangs, they create task forces and hire consultants, streets are paved so they can be dug up again, and as soon as one long-range plan is planned it's time to plan another. As former School Superintendent Ted Drain said on his way out of town, "Nothing is definite in Durham." Our town doesn't have the nickname "Bull City" for nothing.

But the outcome of the flag flap, et al., illustrates one important point about Bull City. Durham is a people's kind of place.

In Durham anyone can call a meeting and someone will show up. Durham is a town where everything happens out in the open, at least for those who pay attention enough to know where open is. Durham does air its dirty laundry in there, but at least some of it does get airing, even if it's at the expense of civic decorum and makes the town look like a joke. All you need in order to appreciate life in Durham is a sense of humor.

Maybe because Durham is so good at being silly, it's touchy about what the neighbors say. In Durham, it's conventional wisdom that Durham has an "image problem," and the problem is so serious that a head of the Convention and Visitors Bureau once recruited an "Image Watch" team to keep track of aspersions cast our way and to set the record straight. The county commissioners once went off to discuss the budget and spent their time talking about image instead. And there were only five of them. This is nothing new, either. In the early twentieth century, a local newspaper, reporting on a young bride's arrival in town, commented that "She might have had a brilliant social career but she came to live in Durham."

Durham has never been able to shake its reputation as a town rough about the edges. The reputation even predates the town, going back to the taverns of Pinhook and Prattsburg, which catered to teamsters hauling freight along the highroad between Hillsborough and Raleigh that ran along the ridge where Durham would rise up. Card-playing, cockfighting, rum-swilling, and ladies of easy virtue made the ridge known as "a roaring old place," according to oral histories; and by the time Durham was incorporated, the saloons outnumbered the churches by a factor of five to one. The town grew fast and rich, with an Old West flavor. Young men were admonished in the press to refrain from spitting tobacco juice in church and a mayor once fined himself for showing up drunk in court.

But Durham has also turned its gritty side into a badge of honor. *Grit* has been a local synonym for *redneck* and *linthead,* but the word also has the connotation of determination, fortitude, and pluck: "True Grit." Years ago, the *Herald-Sun* newspaper instituted an occasional "Durham Grit" award, recognizing some hometown case of determination, fortitude, and pluck on the Saturday editorial page. *Grit* can imply abrasiveness, as in sandpaper, but at the same time it implies a tough and sturdy character.

In the early 1970s, some residents in Trinity Park were awakened by the buzz of chainsaws and found a city crew taking down some of the willow oaks that grace the neighborhood's streets. It turned out that the city authorities intended to blaze a thoroughfare their way, connecting Hillsborough Road with the hoped-to-be revitalized downtown. Now, in those days, decisions on the city's business were typically made in one or another council member's home after Sunday church or in the back room of a steakhouse; but the proto-tree huggers changed that, organizing and going en masse to City Hall to block the thoroughfare despite one councilman's complaint that Durham couldn't stay just "a sleepy little college town." Now, Durham has more than two hundred organized neighborhoods and they still rally for what they want. And sometimes get their way.

Sure, you can't drive three stoplights in a row without getting stopped by at least one, and the streets run every which way except where you need to go—and might change names three times before you realize you should have left all hope at the city limits. We have two Five Points, one a confusing intersection and the other an open-air pharmaceutical exchange. Crime and poverty seem intractable. Slum housing's been an issue at least since 1940. Consultants' reports come and go like colds in kindergarten. The same Durham-raised young lady who exclaimed they were still talking about that flag commented on another occasion, observing citizens and their government in action, "Why are those people acting like that? Don't they know there are children watching?"

It's messy, it's sometimes ugly, more often ridiculous, and it can be a free-for-all. At the same time, it's open to all. In Durham, civic life is a participant sport and everybody's eligible to play. And welcome too. It's as much a part of the community culture as the darkly comic boosterism that, way back in 1913, proclaimed "Durham Renowned the World Around: Health Wealth Progress Success" in 1,230 colored electric light bulbs on a framework atop the telephone exchange building in prime view of passing passenger trains. The lights went on one night during the Christmas shopping season, and one of the very important people speaking to the occasion even likened the "Slogan Sign" to the Star of Bethlehem. Perhaps that was just too much for those on high, perhaps it was just an affront to heavenly good taste, for the Slogan Sign soon went down in a windstorm.

Durham has a sidewalk fiddler who once ran for the United States Senate, and we used to have a panhandler who would give you a quarter if you didn't have one to give him. We had the Lady in White whose touch could cure the sick and crippled, and whose curse could bring quick death — just look at the GI who bumped her without so much as a "Pardon me" and got run down at the next intersection. Or so the legend goes. It's just that kind of a place.

When you are fifteen, it's downright crazy. When you are thirty-five or forty, you might think it absolutely outrageous. A few more years' perspective, it's merely foolish. The fact is, it's just our town being itself and would we really want it any other way? How dull. If you don't like it that way, there are plenty of nearby communities in fifty-seven shades of beige that might suit you better and vice versa. For the rest of us, this is home.

JIM WISE arrived in Durham, sight unseen, as a Duke University freshman in September 1966 and has called Durham home for all but three years since then. He is also a graduate of the Folklore Curriculum at the University of North Carolina at Chapel Hill, where he met Babs, his wife of thirty-five-plus years. Wise has written for Durham newspapers, taught local history at Duke University's Osher Lifelong Learning Institute, and published five books on Durham and regional history.

Feeding on Dreams in Durham

ARIEL DORFMAN

A PLACE OF REFUGE, that is what Durham has ended up being, after a turbulent life: a place where I can work out the contradictions of my existence, find a sort of reconciliation. Perhaps even peace between the two languages that have haunted me, Durham as the place where my English and Spanish cease to war with each other.

But we should be wary of what we wish for.

Take the other night. Sitting at the dinner table with my family, I needed something, *eso*, and I opened my mouth to name it so a member of the family could hand it to me. I waited for the word to come, but nothing, not to the tip of my tongue, not to the stem, not down the throat, and I lingered, expecting one of my two languages to take pity on me, and *nada*, nothing, still nothing, they were ganging up on me.

There I was, *pobrecito*, marooned on this island of speechlessness in the middle of the bustle of Angélica and Rodrigo and his wife Melissa and the little ones, Isabella and Catalina gabbing away, and Joaquín and his girl-friend Robin. My granddaughters are remembering that only a few minutes ago they were climbing Mount Abu, hilariously climbing up and down their *abuelo*/grandpa as if he were the *cordillera* itself, they all have a surfeit of vocabulary at the very instant when a dwarf is drilling a hole in my head, and neither the Spanish that birthed me nor the English that gave me safe haven, neither of my protector/*idiomas* hurries to fill the void even though I'm helplessly married to them both, I almost thirst to again be mono-lingual, simple, elementary.

If I wait any longer the food's going to get cold—and I can't stand my food cold!—so what can I do but point, my finger stretching in the direction that my tongue refuses to go, jerking at the damn thingamasomething, *eso*. I recall a theory of how language started, the sound grunting in hot pursuit of where the index finger was thrusting, and now my sons are into the game. Rodrigo picks up a napkin, "*Esto*, Ariel?" and I shake my head, and "This, Pops?" and that's Joaquín showing me a piece of bread, and they know and I know that what I want is—I'll remember later when it's in my hand—the insignificant salt shaker, *el salero*, but right now all is sudden silence, I can nearly hear the rabbits in our small forest—I always wanted to live in the middle of the woods, and there are turtles and a family of foxes once in a while and snakes and more trilling birds than anyone could identify, wordless creatures who will never find themselves gesticulating at a dinner table, they flow through life like rivers of wonder—I can almost hear the planet turning and the stars being consumed by the furnace of their own light. I am paralyzed, that word I am seeking has disappeared along with all the dictionaries, *el castellano y el inglés* have swallowed each other and reduced me to infancy, suspended me as if time had stopped and space had been abolished, turned me into the target of an Oliver Sacks essay, and if Angélica had not finally shown some mercy and passed me the object in question, pronouncing the word as if I were an idiot or a child learning to speak for the first time, who knows if I would not still be there, a baby, a pre-human mammal, a deaf-mute, waiting, waiting, waiting for the salt of the earth I could not name.

And yet isn't this something to be desired? Both my languages ripening into peaceful coexistence as they age, cohabitating so closely that they can enjoy a good laugh at my expense?

I am beset by the intuition that it was always thus, this mutual aid. It is true that I was born twice, once in Spanish as I fell from my mother's womb in Buenos Aires and once in English when I rose into the winter of New York, and true as well that I can recall neither of those meetings, the day I breathed for the first time and the day when I was so sick I almost stopped breathing. But who can doubt that words were close by, neighboring me on both occasions, greeting me as they have greeted every human on this earth. I don't know what either language said to keep me alive and pacify the dark, but I have lived enough to trust that even back then they were working together and were joined in love for the vast vocabulary of all humanity, I have lived long enough to believe that the origin of life and the origin of language and the origin of poetry are all there, in each first breath of each inhabitant of this planet, each breath as if it were our first, each next breath, the anima, the spirit, what we inspire, what we expire, what separates us from extinction as we inhale and exhale the universe, the simple, almost primeval, arithmetic of breathing in and breathing out.

The written word came later, that effort to make breath everlasting and secure, carve it into rock or ink it on paper or sign it on a screen, so that its cadence can endure beyond us, outlast our lungs, transcend our transitory body and touch someone with its waters. To those waters I have dedicated my existence, calling to those who breathe the same air to also breathe the same verses, with the certainty that we can bridge the gap between bodies and between cultures and between warring parties.

And Durham? Where I live now and from which I will never be exiled, not ever again, except when I die?

Durham in one word?

Home.

And more than one word?

Home at last.

ARIEL DORFMAN's many internationally acclaimed works of poetry, fiction, and nonfiction include his memoirs, *Heading South, Looking North* and *Feeding on Dreams,* from which this essay is adapted. *Death and the Maiden* and his other plays have been staged worldwide. He holds the Walter Hines Page Chair of Literature and Latin American Studies at Duke University. He lives in Durham with Angélica, the wife who has accompanied him through many exiles.

Born and Raised

PIERCE FREELON

I AM THE FIRST MEMBER OF MY FAMILY to be born and raised in Durham, North Carolina. My parents are Yankees, but most people wouldn't be able to tell. My mother's Southern cooking is too good, and a drawl has gradually crept into my father's voice like pollen in spring. My two older siblings were both born in Texas, where my dad was working in the early Eighties. He was a talented and ambitious young architect. By 1983, he had attracted the interest of a Triangle architecture firm. He bundled his family up with his blueprints and sketchbooks, and moved them to Durham.

Around the same time, Dr. Charles Harris was also starting a new job in Durham. He and his colleague, Dr. Ira Smith, founded Harris and Smith Ob-Gyn, and my parents were two of their first clients. Dr. Harris delivered me at Durham Regional Hospital that December. Twenty-five years later, by coincidence or fate, the same Dr. Harris would deliver my son, Justice, at the same hospital. In addition to sharing a genetic signature, we share the same signature on our birth certificates.

How cool is that? We also share the fact that we are the only home-grown Durham boys in our family—and we're proud of it.

Watching Justice navigate Durham triggers flashbacks of my childhood. When I took him to the Museum of Life + Science for the first time, I found myself more engrossed in the experience than he was. I hadn't been there in over a decade, and as he bounced from exhibit to exhibit, I recalled looking at rockets while eating freeze-dried astronaut ice cream. I remembered believing, with all of my heart, that the mechanical dinosaurs nestled between plastic ferns and boulders were real—especially the ancient brontosaurs which peeked out at me from the wooded canopy on Murray Avenue. Everything from the tornado simulator to the sound garden to Loblolly Park with its handpumps and leaky faucets flooded my mind with fond memories of Durham past.

I wondered how Justice was perceiving the museum and if it would have the same lasting impact on him. I wanted to tell him to appreciate it—to soak in the vibe and relish it because there was no place else like Durham in the world. But I didn't push it. After all, Justice was only three and I was caught between the rock of nostalgia and the hard place of melodrama.

I think I am so passionate about encouraging Justice to appreciate his birthplace because it took me so long to do the same. As a toddler, I loved exploring the museum, going on shaded strolls through Eno River trails, and sitting behind first base at Durham Bulls games. However, as an adolescent I became apathetic, probably par for the course for most tweens. By the time I finished middle school, I was over Durham.

Durham had become like a platonic girlfriend I had loved, trusted, and known my entire life, but wasn't ready to date. I was more interested in courting more exotic cities—the sandy shores of Myrtle Beach or Charlotte with its Hornets and skyscrapers. After my freshman year of high school, I jumped at the opportunity to see what else was out there. I left Durham School of the Arts to attend a boarding school in the mountains of Western Massachusetts. Nearly seven hundred miles away from anything that resembled home, I had a blast gallivanting with the New Englanders. Even so, the experience actually made me appreciate Durham more. I discovered I preferred collard greens to clam chowder, ACC basketball to NHL hockey, and Southern hospitality to New England reserve.

After high school I hopped, skipped, and jumped up I-40 to enroll at the University of North Carolina at Greensboro. From a city standpoint, this proved to be an error in judgment. The 'Boro was full of miles upon miles of strip malls, which scarred the city's main arteries like unwanted tattoos. The redundancy of services in each strip mall was staggering—CVS catty-cornered to Rite Aid, Olive Garden across from Carrabba's, and Walmart in the same plaza with Target. It made me miss Durham's small businesses that employ a diverse array of Triangle residents and entrepreneurs.

After two years as a Spartan, I transferred to the University of North Carolina at Chapel Hill—a risky maneuver. Chapel Hill is beautiful and has more money than Durham. To extend the Durham-as-platonic-friend metaphor, Chapel Hill is the prom queen of the Triangle. However, my years at Chapel Hill only strengthened my bond with Durham, in part because of Chapel Hillians' disdain for their neighbor to the east. One might expect that contempt to be rooted in the Carolina/Duke rivalry. But to many UNC students, Duke and Durham were separate entities, equally despicable for entirely different reasons. Defending Durham to my UNC classmates became a daily chore. I became adept at articulating Durham's many fine attributes. Words are powerful. The more I talked up Durham, the more I developed a deep and sincere appreciation for it.

When I graduated from UNC, I accepted a fellowship at Syracuse University. Syracuse was *frigid*. I took advantage of every opportunity to sprint home and thaw out in the Bull City. After years of digging out of lake-effect snow I was more than ready to come home.

When the fellowship ended, I found myself at a crossroads.

I had an awesome job offer in the Triangle—a teaching position at my alma mater, UNC at Chapel Hill, a dream gig for me. On the other hand, I had an amazing opportunity to coordinate the Bebop to Hip Hop program for the Thelonious Monk Institute of Jazz in Los Angeles. If there was one city in the country that could make me think twice about moving back to Durham it was Los Angeles, a completely foreign and exciting city at the epicenter of popular culture. It was a once-in-a-lifetime offer that I couldn't refuse. And it was the right decision. Committing to a city is similar to committing to a serious relationship. Before settling down with the one for life, it's sometimes a good idea to explore other options. The Thelonious Monk Institute of Jazz was originally scheduled to set up shop in Durham, back in the early 1980s. It was not without irony that their job offer uprooted me from Durham as well.

We were only in Los Angeles for a few months when my wife and I became pregnant. All of a sudden the flashing lights and Cali charisma wore thin. Everything was being weighed against the benefits of our child growing up in the family-oriented spiritual womb of Durham. After little discussion, we were on the first thing smoking back home. With both our immediate families in Durham, our homecoming was sweeter than slow-cooked Carolina barbecue.

I arrived in Durham much like my father had, twenty-five years prior — a hungry and skilled artist with family in tow. I matured over the years, and was able to appreciate home even more, having lived in other corners of the country.

While I was gone, Durham had matured as well. The home base, which I brushed off in high school, had developed into a brick house, with all the amenities of the cities I ditched it for *and then some.* As a young father I earned the dual privilege of being both a Durham explorer and ambassador. I relished revealing Durham's secrets to Justice, only to learn new riddles for us to unravel together. I only hope that he learns to grab the Bull by its horns and, despite the allure of other cities, hold on with all his strength.

PIERCE FREELON is a musician, writer, and artivist (artist-activist) with a passion for creativity and community. He is front man of the genre-bending The Beast, hailed as a "natural, engaging blend of jazz and hip hop," by *Jazz Times Magazine.* He has taught music, African American studies, and political science at the University of North Carolina at Chapel Hill and North Carolina Central University. A lifelong Durham resident, he does not plan on moving, ever.

Home Again

ADAM SOBSEY

THOMAS WOLFE GAVE IT THE ALIAS OF EXETER and called it a "dreary tobacco town." He sends his protagonist, Eugene Gant, to a Durham slum to lose his virginity to a prostitute. Although this is a young city, less than a hundred and fifty years old, it has never been innocent. It was built on tobacco, of course.

The tobacco is gone, but the dreariness has abided. In her first and only novel, *Wonder When You'll Miss Me*, the late Amanda Davis renames her hometown "Gleryton"—like a cross between *dreary* and *glum*—and then grants her morose protagonist permission to escape Durham in a burst of giddy, almost gleeful violence.

I escaped, too. When I left Durham I was eighteen, just like Eugene Gant in *Look Homeward, Angel* when he left Asheville. Whether Wolfe was right that You Can't Go Home Again, I had no intention of returning. His dictum was inert for me.

But another way of putting it hit home. Late in the 1988 movie *Bull Durham*, which made the city famous and hangs over its consciousness just as the sweet, sharp aroma of curing tobacco once did, the young phenom pitcher Nuke LaLoosh gets called up to the Show, the major leagues. He's been carrying on all summer long with Annie Savoy, the seasoned Durham Bulls groupie who selects one ballplayer per year as a consort.

Nuke is naive, gifted, and hopeful, a *prospect* in multiple senses of the word; but Annie, played by Susan Sarandon, is older, sadder, and wiser. After he learns of his promotion to the big leagues, Nuke tells Annie he'll be back to see her again soon. She replies, with tender condescension: "Honey, when you leave Durham, you don't come back."

That's true in Hollywood but not in Durham. The Bulls set me straight — not the cinema Bulls, the *real* Durham Bulls. I worked for the team in my formative years. Actually, that isn't strictly true. I was never on the Bulls' payroll. In the first season I worked there, I received no compensation at all except a free sandwich and a Coke in the fifth inning. The second year, I got five cash dollars per game, in addition to the food. But it was a dream job. I sat next to the Durham Bulls radio broadcaster and "assisted" him (he paid me out of his own pocket). I had the best seat in the house at shabby but charming Durham Athletic Park (the DAP), a World War II relic, refurbished in 1980 for minor league baseball, which had been absent from Durham for a decade.

It was the last age here of unsmoothed edges and oddball baseball — Duke graduate students and smoky, toothless old-timers alike got drunk in the crowded bleachers where mischievous kids smashed praying mantises for fun, all under the din of the profanely accelerating rally chant: "Bulls' hit! Bulls'hit! Bullshit!" You could smell the tobacco and see the nighthawks in the air and listen to foul balls smash car windows in the parking lot. And you could watch Brad Komminsk. Anyone who was around the DAP back then remembers Komminsk. Like Nuke LaLoosh, he was a can't-miss phenom — he nearly won the Carolina League Triple Crown in 1981. Komminsk was our king.

I grew up at the DAP, crookedly. I watched a lot of failure, which is mostly what the play-by-play of baseball is. The Bulls weren't very good back then, and during the occasional seasons when they were, they weren't good enough. The franchise was in Class A, low in the Atlanta Braves' farm system, and most of the players had no shot at the major leagues. The ones who did weren't here long, and, as Annie Savoy foresaw, they didn't come back to Durham after they left.

I learned to recognize the difference between a prospect and a suspect, and to understand that the difference didn't always express itself in statistical results. I learned how grindingly, punishingly hard baseball is to play, which allowed me to appreciate the difficulty of almost all worthwhile pursuits. I learned about cultural difference, as I watched Latino players try to make sense of their temporary new home (though they knew they were never going to fit in). I learned some strange, advanced stuff about sex from hanging around ballplayers. I learned about trust via its opposite, betrayal, when my stepfather—who had initiated me into what Annie Savoy called "the Church of Baseball" at the DAP—left the family for another woman. He and his new groupie didn't last much longer than Annie and Nuke, and like Nuke he left Durham and didn't come back.

Thus the DAP, and Durham, was a great place to grow up, because you *really* grew up: You got older, sadder, and wiser like Annie and the man she's really made for and finds in the end, Crash Davis, the journeyman catcher in *Bull Durham* played by Kevin Costner. Durham had none of Chapel Hill's prettiness or Raleigh's capital bigness. Durham was, well, a little *glery*, yet also honest and mild—like the DAP, worn and warped but hospitable. Politically it was (and still is) way to the left, but amiably so, with a *laissez-faire* tolerance for whoever you were and whatever you wanted to do. The defunct, desolate downtown of the 1980s was made of carious, exhausted brick. The old American Tobacco complex was a ruin, like an ancient temple. Adults and teenagers alike put on plays in bat-infested former hat shops near Five Points, and afterward the teenagers sneaked cigarettes on the roof of the Corcoran Street parking deck. Forever, it seemed, Durham never had a decent bar.

Fifteen years after I left Durham, having lived all over the U.S. and traveled widely overseas, I came back. I had no purpose in returning and no intention to stay long, but it was 2003, and within a decade, the city would be transformed. Downtown reawoke. Old buildings got new life, often in the form of good places to eat and drink. A scrappy, DIY entrepreneurship — a Bullishness, you could say — seems uniquely Durham. "I think that may be one of the keys to Durham's success," says Jean Bradley Anderson, who wrote our definitive history and has lived here since 1955. "There's always been opportunity here for whatever you're interested in."

The Durham Bulls have been transformed, as well. In the 1990s, they were sold, moved out of the dilapidated DAP and into Durham Bulls Athletic Park, a new ballpark built next to the renovated American Tobacco complex (DPAC, a performing arts center, popped up adjacent to it a few years ago, too). The team changed its major-league affiliation: They signed on with the brand new, innovative Tampa Bay Rays and moved up to Triple-A, the level right below the major leagues. Now, most of the Bulls' roster has major-league experience, and every season brings an established big-leaguer here temporarily on injury rehab. The Rays have one of the best farm systems in baseball, and with their players the Durham Bulls have made it to the playoffs for five straight years. The Bulls are booming. And as the Bulls go, Durham goes.

I've had close contact with both the team and the city, covering the Bulls and their milieu for the last few years. I, too, have been transformed: I have become a sportswriter (and a grownup). But in the spirit of Durham, I do it my way, cranking out 3,000–word postgame essays late into the sticky night. Just as Durham was a great place to grow up, it is a good place to be a grownup, too. You can do, make, be what you want here. You can, like the modern-day Bulls, be *almost* major-league.

At the new DBAP, which isn't really that new anymore, I even got to see the great Brad Komminsk again. The former Bulls superstar, a first-round draft pick in 1979, never succeeded in the Show. He bounced around, like Crash Davis, from team to team, struggling with all of them, battling injuries, before calling it quits after a disappointing career. Afterward, he went into coaching. For a while he *did* Go Home Again, managing a couple of baseball teams in Ohio, his native state, before joining the Baltimore Orioles organization. Last year, he was the batting coach for their Triple-A team, the Norfolk Tides, who roll into Durham to take on the Bulls a few times each season.

Komminsk, who turned fifty years old in 2011, was almost unrecognizable. He looked haggard, out of shape, joyless, grudging, defeated. He made caustic comments in the coaches' office after games. I wanted to tell him that I knew how great he had been, so that he would know that his greatness, though gone, was not forgotten. But it didn't seem right to intrude on his past that way. "We can't turn life back to the hours when our lungs were sound, our blood hot, our bodies young," Wolfe writes in *Look Homeward, Angel*. "We are three-cents-worth of lime and iron. . . ." Decades later, in *Bull Durham*, Crash Davis echoes Wolfe, lamenting that his aging body is "worth seven cents a pound."

One does not want to be forced to look back (or homeward). Wolfe again: ". . . he was like a man who stands upon a hill above the town he has left, yet does not say 'The town is near,' but turns his eyes upon the distant soaring ranges." One must resist the pull of nostalgia, and live life forward. Durham is a much better place to live now than it was in Eugene Gant's childhood, and in mine, in every way.

Some of the old things persist, though, including the old Durham Athletic Park, and in the best of ways. The Bulls are no longer tenants, but hundreds of baseball games are still played there every season, by colleges, high schools, and others—the Bulls themselves have played two souvenir games there since 2010. Umpires have trained there, too. "Work was the new morality," Jean Bradley Anderson writes in *Durham County*, and the old DAP is still working, still as moral as the great game which is played there. The Durham Bulls franchise now operates the old ballpark as well as their new one, less than a mile away. And that's exactly right: They have one arm working in the past, and one in the present. Or, as the great catcher Roy Campanella put it, "You gotta be a man to play baseball for a living, but you gotta have a lot of little boy in you too."

ADAM SOBSEY is a playwright, sportswriter, and essayist. He has covered the Durham Bulls for the *Independent Weekly* since 2009. His plays have been performed in New York, California, Texas, and North Carolina. He lives in downtown Durham.

49

The Morning After Amendment One

BARRY YEOMAN

IF YOU DIDN'T PEEK AT THE NUMBERS on the TV inside—where Amendment One was racking up a 22-point margin of victory—you might have imagined the scene outside Fullsteam Brewery in Durham was a celebration that election night. The air was thick with grilled cheese and Korean tacos, punctuated by cheers from Motorco Music Hall across the street and even a rowdy parade. On a patch of grass, the Bulltown Strutters and Blue-Tailed Skinks were blowing their trombones and clarinet, shaking their hips and a tambourine, as if the passage to a better world depended on it. *My flag boy and your flag boy / Sitting by the fire / My flag boy says to your flag boy / I'm gonna set your flag on fire.* Listening to the musicians singing "Iko Iko" made me feel like we were at a secondline jazz funeral, squeezing out every bit of available life at the moment of deepest loss.

We drank strong beer and reminded ourselves how far we've come in the past few decades, and how things often get ugliest before the biggest leaps forward. We quoted Martin Luther King Jr.: "The arc of the moral universe is long, but it bends toward justice." But Lord, we asked in our exhaustion, couldn't it just bend a wee bit faster? I thought back to the first time I found myself singing festive songs during a moment of defeat. It was thirty years ago. I was sitting in the back of a paddy wagon.

In November 1981, a committee of the New York City Council was deciding whether to outlaw discrimination against lesbians and gay men. I was dispatched to cover the thirteen hours of hearings for three neighborhood weeklies. I was a twenty-one-year-old college student with long hair and a skinny reporter's notebook, and I was filled with journalism-school conviction that we were supposed to serve as neutral observers of the day's events.

For two days I took notes as opponents warned of both lawlessness and heavenly retribution if the gay-rights bill passed. They peppered their speeches with what one council member called "enough quotations from the Scriptures for many months of Sundays." Evangelist Joanne Highley promised a slippery slope: "Give them rights," she said, "and then there will come the rights of those who want to have sex with animals. And then there will come the rights of those who want to stand alone and have sex with trees." (An activist jumped up and shouted, "I'm going up to Central Park to cruise a black oak!") At the mention of a recent machine-gun attack on a gay bar that left two men dead, Heshy Friedman of the Jewish Moral Committee applauded and chanted, "Good, good." But there were also brave acts of self-disclosure, most notably by a police sergeant named Charles Cochrane. His very presence rebutted a union official who claimed not to know a single gay cop.

Just before the vote, Council President Carol Bellamy spread her billow-sleeved arms on the dais and quoted William Faulkner's *Intruders in the Dust*. "Some things you must always be unable to bear," she said. "Some things you must never stop refusing to bear. Injustice and outrage and dishonor and shame. No matter how young you are or how old you have got. Not for kudos and not for cash; your picture in the paper nor money in the bank either. Just refuse to bear them."

The committee voted 6-3 to kill the civil rights bill. I surprised myself by standing up and moving toward the front of the chambers. Protestors were forming a circle on the floor, and just for the night I shed my journalistic detachment. Over the next four hours, we told one another our stories and sang "We Shall Not Be Moved" (of course). We took our own vote on the bill, approving it 26-0. Several council members kept vigil with us, one weeping openly. We were not allowed to use the bathrooms, and finally a police officer told us to leave under orders from Mayor Ed Koch. When twenty-one of us refused, we were arrested for trespassing.

I graduated and left New York a few months later and have lived in North Carolina for the past twenty-seven years. My life here—as a professional, a homeowner, a husband, an AARP member—bears little resemblance to my undergraduate days. Yet watching Amendment One roll to victory, I couldn't help but flash back to 1981.

Why should that be? After all, the intervening decades have taken us far from the culture of "sex with trees." ACT UP. Rock Hudson. *Will & Grace.* Holocaust memorials. Gay-straight student alliances. Civil unions. *Philadelphia.* Barney Frank. *Lawrence v. Texas,* which legalized consensual gay relationships. Ads for JC Penney and McDonald's. Ellen DeGeneres. Anti-bullying campaigns. Rachel Maddow. "Don't Ask, Don't Tell" and its repeal. Elton John. Craigslist. David Sedaris. "It's Raining Men." In many localities, antidiscrimination laws feel old hat. Ten countries and eight U.S. states have voted to marry same-sex couples. Every poll, indeed every conversation, shows that we are one generation away from when homosexuality will shed its political relevance. President Barack Obama, Vice President Joe Biden, and Education Secretary Arne Duncan are just the latest prominent officials to throw their support behind marriage equality.

In Durham, where I live, lesbians and gay men are so fully integrated into civic life that sexual orientation (at least to me) feels like an afterthought.

My friends, who are overwhelmingly straight, think of my husband and me not as a gay couple, but as a couple. My election precinct voted 95 percent against the amendment. Even my Republican friends opposed the measure, and went out of their ways to tell me so.

Given the relative ease with which I navigate my world as a gay man, I've been trying to understand my feelings over the past few weeks, which run less toward anger or fear and more toward weariness. It's not about Amendment One in particular: With notable exceptions, the homophobic rhetoric has been relatively muted this time around. Rather, it's about the corrosive effect of three decades of adulthood in which I've never once assumed that I'd ever be entitled to the most basic rights of citizenship.

Last year in Massachusetts, a gruff-voiced judge signed a waiver of the three-day waiting period normally required for marriage there. The courthouse employees congratulated us as we left the building. But even after a town clerk signed our marriage certificate, we didn't acquire a single one of the 1,100-plus federal rights given to opposite-sex couples, and our wedding was functionally invalidated when our plane landed in North Carolina. (I joked to my mother that she has a legal son-in-law in her home state, but I don't have a legal husband in mine.) We have a passel of notarized papers that might or might not help us in the event of a medical catastrophe. But no document will give us, for example, automatic inheritance or spousal Social Security benefits.

Surely, every gay man or lesbian copes differently with the knowledge that the liberties that form the very essence of American democracy remain outside our grasp. For me, the mechanism is something akin to journalistic distancing. When I'm reporting on a story—talking with Louisiana oystermen after the BP oil spill, or watching residents tear down an abandoned house in a Detroit neighborhood—I am fully engaged in the moment, but through a lens of otherness: *This is your world. It is not mine.* Other journalists put down that lens when they come home. I never fully do. I attend a friend's heterosexual wedding; talk at a party with someone who volunteers with his son's Boy Scout troop; or receive an invitation to donate blood during a drive—and find myself viewing all those experiences as out-side to my own. Then I generalize to other things, because it has become a habit. *This is your world. It is not mine.*

This sense that many of these basic rituals are available to others but not to me can't help but alter my relationship to *civitas*. Self-identify-ing as American is predicated on some elemental expectations: I can bind my financial life to another's. I can volunteer my time to help foster our community's youth. I can volunteer my healthy blood to save a life. Take away these basic assumptions, and patriotism means very little. Funny, but I don't get angry when I think of this, or even sad. It just is.

Multiply me by a few million, and think about how much civic energy is squandered as a result.

On Election morning, I left my house at 4:30 AM and walked through my neighborhood toward downtown. In yard after yard, I passed blue-and-white cardboard signs opposing the amendment. A hand-painted sign nailed to a telephone pole read, *NO ON ONE.*

Many of my neighbors had arrived at CCB Plaza before me. The local NBC affiliate was filming its early-morning show there, featuring everyone from Wool E. Bull to the North Carolina Central University marching band to the Monuts Donuts tricyclist. The Strutters and Skinks were there as well, jamming off-camera. The Only Burger and Pie Pushers trucks slung break-fast; the latter displayed a handbill saying, *Another Food Truck AGAINST Amendment One.* A couple dozen Durhamites holding anti-amendment banners and picket signs formed the backdrop for the two-and-a-half-hour broadcast. Durham's consensus was evident, and it was thrilling.

This has been the redemptive aspect of this struggle. I have never seen a community mount such a forceful, unified, creative response to a collective threat. I have never had so many neighbors tell me, "Your battle is mine too." The results of that Tuesday's election might solidify the sense of otherness with which I view my state and country. But my patriotism to my city has never been stronger.

BARRY YEOMAN moved to Durham in 1985 to work for the *Independent Weekly*. He is now a freelance magazine journalist and radio documentarian and has written recently for the *American Prospect, AARP The Magazine, Audubon, Good Housekeeping, OnEarth*, and *O, The Oprah Magazine*. His website is barryyeoman.com.

In the Gardens Beside a Library

JAMES APPLEWHITE

JAMES APPLEWHITE is the author of eleven books of poetry, including *A Diary of Altered Light* and *Quartet for Three Voices*. Emeritus Professor of English at Duke University, he has received numerous awards, including the American Academy and Institute of Arts and Letters Jean Stein Award in Poetry, a Guggenheim Fellowship, and the North Carolina Award in Literature.

The willow oak has written in it
an ink of time-underlayment.
I say the word *emeritus*
and the wind-rubbed coppery surface
touches my eyes like a worn rug.
Corded by limbs to a base in soil
it recovers those years of toil
that layered other leaves in another place.
The library's vellum and coffee still drug
my memory, like Gothic walls and trees above.
There I and my gnarled masters strove,
limning interpretive cursives and dots
onto the passionate dead's still living arguments.

There wide-browed Lionel carried his satchel
into the crenellated tower, kindly, impersonal
and shone his lamp through a diamonded
window, out toward me, where I read
my fortune through the screening tree
and fed ideals on its shadowy history.

The fortress-like place of these pasts,
standing behind me, casts
no shade on my course
where free in the twilight I pass
the labeled species, these knowledge-trees —
not reading, and with no remorse.

As I walk farther on
one orange-green golden
final maple says that vision
is wisdom, that beauty is changing
and is its own meaning.
This space of time is at last my own.

Friends & Neighbors

Shirley's Garden

An Oral History

DAVID CECELSKI

BETWEEN 1998 AND 2008 I wrote an oral history series called
"Listening to History" for the Sunday edition of the Raleigh *News*
& Observer. With the support of the Southern Oral History Program at the
University of North Carolina at Chapel Hill, I traveled across the state, listening to stories and recording a mosaic of voices about North Carolina's
past. As part of the project, I talked with Allan Troxler, who worked in the
garden behind the Blevins House, which at that time was a group residence
in Durham for people with HIV/AIDS.

A Greensboro native, Allan had started this bountiful garden eight
years earlier to provide produce and cut flowers for the residents and their
caregivers. We walked down dense rows of sunflowers and okra, beneath
seven-foot-high trellises of tomatoes and cucumber, alongside lush patches
of watermelon and cantaloupe. Allan had been a volunteer at Blevins
House since it was founded in the mid-Eighties by a group of his friends,
organized as the AIDS Community Residence Association.

Many of his closest friends have died during the AIDS epidemic,
including his longtime partner, Carl Wittman, in 1986. Like so many other
Tar Heel volunteers and families, he responded to the AIDS epidemic by
quietly taking care of the small things that one person can do for another
to make life more bearable, more decent. He nursed the ill, made endear-
ing keepsakes — and tended the garden.

Allan began by telling me the story of the person who inspired him
to start the garden:

> Shirley was an old mountain woman. I think she might have gotten
> HIV from prostitution. When she came to the house, which is a very
> pleasant, middle-class ranch home, she just sat on the edge of the sofa
> for about a month. Like she was just waiting for the Greyhound to take
> her back to the hills — she was so ill at ease in what to her was this pala-
> tial home. I suspect she had only lived in little cabins and trailers. But she
> took to lining the porch with coffee cans full of houseplants. She was
> turning it into home.
>
> Shirley was real deadpan. When she was joking, you couldn't tell
> because she wouldn't smile, but then you'd see that her eyes were
> flashing. Didn't have many teeth. She dipped snuff and had a snuff can.
> Most all of her hair was gone. I had no idea how old she was. She
> looked ancient, but I remember at some point seeing her age and I was
> surprised at how much younger she was than I thought.
>
> We all knew that Shirley loved plants. Her birthday was on May the
> first, and so everybody gave her houseplants. I gave her a few seed packets.
> That's how the garden got started. The first year the garden was just a little
> patch with some zinnias and a few other things. Shirley would sit up on the
> porch — she didn't have any energy to work in the yard — and she'd boss
> me around. The residence is housing of last resort. It's for people who
> can't find anywhere else to live. Anyway, that first year the garden was for
> Shirley. And I planted her zinnias, because they were so colorful.

She probably came here through the HIV/AIDS clinic at Duke. They refer most of the residents to the house. At that point—1989— there probably weren't adequate services up there in the mountains for her. The clinics at Duke and Carolina both handle clients from all over the state. Blevins House, and several other residences in the area, are pretty cosmopolitan. Often times it's people from all over the state.

Shirley took great pride in the garden. By fall, we had all kinds of beautiful things in bloom. In October, we planned an excursion to the State Fair with Shirley and other folks from the house. It was the first time she had ever been to anything like the State Fair. She was tremendously excited. We got Shirley over there in a wheelchair, all made up, in her bouffant wig. Along with J.R. and Tony, who was Lumbee.

So we've been there maybe ten minutes. We're right in front of the turkey shoot on the midway. The rifles all go off. Straightaway, Shirley goes into a grand mal seizure, which I had never dealt with at all. It was terrifying. She went white and rigid. Fortunately, Tony had had seizures as a complication from AIDS. He had a sense of what to do.

We wheeled Shirley over to the Red Cross booth. It ended up I had to bring her back out here. As she was coming to, about when we were back to Durham, she said: "Where are we? How come we're not at the State Fair?" And I said: "Shirley you had a seizure. I got to take you home." She was just furious, because she had been looking forward to this for weeks. I was feeling really bad, thinking, God, what can we do for Shirley?

The next morning, I came out to the garden, and there were these coxcombs, which are great big flowers—deep, deep pink and red—that look like rooster's combs. They'd been off in a corner and once or twice I dumped Miracle-Gro on them and otherwise I had ignored them. So I thought, well, there's another round of the flower competition at the fair. I'll take these coxcombs over.

A couple days later, a friend and I went by the flower show, and there were the coxcombs covered with ribbons. First prize! Best of show!

These huge, apricot-colored ribbons with three or four tiers of ruffles. It was perfect. So I bought Shirley a State Fair sweatshirt and we pinned on all the ribbons and brought it back to her. She was tickled. It wasn't all the same as being there, but it was next best. She died that next spring.

Shirley, Ken, now Roosevelt—those are the three faces the garden has most assumed for me. Ken loved the garden. He had grown up at an orphanage at Chalybeate Springs. They made the kids do field work—I think it was a strawberry farm—so he had this almost instinctive relationship to the garden. He was here for a couple years. Early on, it was rare that anybody was here for that long. It's changed now. With these new drugs and drug combinations, people are living a lot longer.

Last fall, Roosevelt started coming out and puttering around, chopping weeds, clearing beds. Now he's gaunt and doesn't have much energy. He's on oxygen twenty-four hours a day, but he has a portable tank so he can come preside. I tell him he's our patron saint. So many people, once they're diagnosed, give up. He has no patience with that. He's from Durham, but he worked in New York, polishing diamonds at Tiffany's.

Especially in those early years, I think the benefits of volunteerism were at least as much for the volunteers as for the people who lived here. We all needed reassurance. We all needed some sense of, well, there is something I can do. Everybody felt defeated. I think all of us were searching for a way to understand this very natural process, this epidemic, as something other than this terrible judgment, this holocaust, this tragedy. I've hoped that here, in the garden, is some solace in the cycles of life, death, and then regeneration. . . .

And maybe to have a vase of zinnias or a sack of okra matters in a small way.

Historian and folklorist **DAVID CECELSKI** is the author of several award-winning books, including *The Waterman's Song: Slavery and Freedom in Maritime North Carolina; Along Freedom Road: Hyde County, North Carolina, and the Fate of Black Schools in the South;* and *A Historian's Coast.* His latest book is *The Fire of Freedom: Abraham Galloway and the Slaves' Civil War.* This view is adapted from a story that originally appeared in the Raleigh *News & Observer.*

Fifth Avenue

(for Durham's June Hamilton, my pops)

SHIRLETTE AMMONS

Owning its sheen,
the Chrysler key dangles
in the trunk's slit
the luster sells itself to me
one shiny emblem to another

It's a eighty-six. Only fifty thousand miles,
He brags.
He is the biggest wide-mouth in Scott's Pond.
I am his tossed-back minnow.

How many Durham's darkies
been hauled to heaven
in this chariot?
I ask,
my eyes crawling through the trunk

We laugh in mirror images
I am his half-boy, half-mechanic
our snickers like a snare
burst through same teeth,
whole faces shake

SHIRLETTE AMMONS is a poet, writer, musician, and youth arts coordinator at the ArtsCenter in Carrboro. She is a Cave Canem Fellow and has written reviews and articles for the *Independent Weekly*, Duke Performances' blog, *The Thread*, and other publications. Her second collection of poetry, *Matching Skin* (Carolina Wren Press), features an introduction by Nikky Finney, 2011 National Book Award winner for Poetry. Her recent musical collaboration with the Dynamite Brothers, *And Lovers Like,* is available at www.shirletteammons.com.

El Nuevo South

RODRIGO DORFMAN

TO MY SURPRISE I returned from a short trip not long ago to find my neighbors' house deserted. I have no idea what happened to them. Even though they lived across the street, I can't say I really knew them all that well. I knew their names and that they were from Guerrero, Mexico. Sometimes I would smile and wave to them from the window of my car on my way to work. Other times I would walk by their house with my daughter and say hello and exchange pleasantries standing on their porch, taking refuge from North Carolina's scorching sun. We would talk in Spanish about the Latino Credit Union, soccer, the best place to buy tomatillos, about their hopes and dreams and sometimes nightmares.

The truth is they were what some refer to as illegals, which is another way of saying criminals in the eye of the law. How did I know this? They trusted me with their secret and with the story of their journey across the desert—how they walked, how they were lost, how they prayed, how one night they had to literally dive into a thicket of thorn bushes to hide from a menacing helicopter. The scars on their arms and on the cheek of one of their children were still there, proof of their sacrifice. I wanted to know. I wanted to be a witness. For me, a sense of place was bound by the act of becoming a willing accomplice to their crime. This complicity increased my endearment and compassion toward them, for it reminded me of my own past. It reminded me of how far I had come as an immigrant and how far others still had to go.

Ever since I left Chile as a child, I've been looking for a home—a piece of earth, a peace of mind, a place where my memories can rest for a while beneath the shade of a tree I have planted, in a garden I have cultivated, under the roof of a house I can call my own. I left with my family one month after the military coup of September 11, 1973, that destroyed our country's democracy. With not much more than a stuffed rabbit in one arm, holding on to my mother's hand, I was dragged into exile, seduced by the thrill of flying on airplanes and visiting faraway places, reassured that I would soon return, very soon, to see my friends, my family, my toys, my country. For a whole decade after we left Chile, we lived out of suitcases. Always on the go, we lived in Paris, Amsterdam, Maryland, dozens of houses and apartments; so much so, we didn't even own a mattress.

And so, I was always the one leaving behind unfinished friends, vistas, and gardens. Now that I have finally settled down in Durham, I've begun to enjoy what was denied me all those years: a view from a window I can recognize day after day, for years to come. It's a soothing and reassuring thought and yet . . . and yet today as I look out my window and see that my neighbors are gone—their children no longer dangerously bicycling in the middle of the street and the sometimes-loud Ranchero music no longer blasting from one of their cars—I feel my sense of security slightly shattered. And to think that they had just laid out some paving stones in front of their muddy entrance and planted beautiful little pink flowers along side them!

Maybe belonging demands that we constantly test our sense of security by choosing to intervene in the lives of others. A few days before my trip, I was shopping at my local thrift store when I heard an all-too-familiar sound. The sales clerk, a middle-aged Anglo woman, was gently butchering the Spanish language in an honest attempt to communicate with two non-English–speaking Latinos. I say a familiar sound, because in Durham this kind of intercultural linguistic connection is the stuff of everyday life. No matter where I go — the supermarket, the DMV, the mall, a yard sale — I find myself frequently acting as translator, even mediator between my two cultures. Being bilingual carries with it a heavy responsibility. Sometimes, it demands that you intervene and enter private worlds; other times it allows you to stay on the margins and observe, so to speak, the complex meanderings of a culture in the making.

But that day my conscience pushed me to intervene. I stepped in and translated to the two Latinos what the Anglo woman was trying to say. Apparently, another man, someone they knew, the store clerk assumed, had already paid for the pants one of the Latinos wanted to buy. It was a gift.

The Latinos gave me a disconcerted look, and shook their heads in disbelief. They knew no one there. "Vinimos solos," we came alone, they told me, in that quiet and unassuming tone so common among Meso-American Indians. I could tell they were beginning to feel apprehensive, as if someone had been spying on them, as if a dark cloud was about to descend upon their heads. After a few more confusing exchanges, the woman finally figured out that the mysterious man did not really know them and had bought them the pants as an act of charity.

The people standing on line at the register behind us were now watching the scene, adding to the uneasiness of the situation. I paused for a moment to consider the weight of my words, hoping to not further embarrass the two Latinos. I took a deep breath and explained the situation. I told them that it was a gift from a stranger. This time they shook their heads, not in confusion, but with that strong sense of dignity so central to the survival of Latin American indigenous cultures. They put the pants down on the register. With a slight trace of anger in their voice, they told me they couldn't accept the gift and walked out.

I was left with a bitter taste in my mouth as I tried to imagine the intentions of the anonymous giver whose deed of charity had been interpreted as an act of racist paternalism. How can it be, I asked myself, that a gift can sometimes do more harm than good? How can attempts to communicate turn into a reason to alienate? This situation, at first glance, seems far removed from our daily experience. After all, we rarely give anonymous gifts, or for that matter receive them. And yet, something in that moment resonated deeply.

The mysterious samaritan was giving without truly knowing those he wanted to help. He was imagining them as he wished them to be, rather than trying to find out who they really were. What they really needed. The truth is that we all make this mistake in our lives. We hold on to our preconceptions and are unable to open our arms and receive others different than ourselves. We don't give. We impose. It's a dangerous mindset, especially when it becomes, albeit unconsciously, the cornerstone from where many of us build a sense of community.

Still, I can't help myself. As a writer I live to imagine the lives of others, a world inhabited as much by their absence as by their presence. As I look out my window at the empty house where my neighbors once lived I can't help wondering, What happened to them? Did one of them lose a job and they were forced to move to an even smaller house; or are they doing just fine and actually moved to a larger one? Or did one of them get caught without their papers? And what would happen to the children? Or did they just simply "move" on? They often told me how much they liked it here in Durham, the work, the weather, and the friendly neighborhood. For years I was the one who left in the middle of the night like a wandering immigrant and now I was the one that had to witness the disappearance of others. Now I wished I had taken the time to visit them a bit more and in turn invite their children to play in my yard and share with them the vision of a future where they wouldn't have to live like criminals because they didn't possess the correct piece of paper. After all, you can't always bathe in your own blessings. Maybe that's what belonging truly means. To be able to get out of those comforting waters and let others revel in them.

RODRIGO DORFMAN is an award-winning filmmaker and multimedia producer who has worked with POV and the BBC. His films have been screened at film festivals around the world, including those in Toronto, Edinburgh, Telluride, and Durham. He won the 2011 Jury Award for Best Short at the Full Frame Documentary Film Festival. His next feature, *Occupy the Imagination: Tales of Seduction and Resistance,* will be released in late 2012.

The Food on My Porch

SIDNEY CRUZE

LAST SUMMER, a friend introduced me to his girlfriend, and as we said hello, he told me she rode her bike to my house every week. For a second I wondered how she knew where I lived. Then it clicked.

"Oh right," I said. "The CSA."

Our house has been the Durham drop point for Maple Spring Gardens Community Supported Agriculture (CSA) shares since 2004. The farm's CSA program allows members to pay up front for a share of produce that is delivered weekly during growing season. So every Tuesday, April through September, Maple Spring brings about sixty boxes of produce and four buckets of flowers to our front porch.

We live in an old neighborhood, where some houses have porches, but many do not. Ours is not large, just seven by sixteen, but all the CSA boxes fit in stacks of six, with room left over for people. Over the years about five hundred Maple Spring CSA subscribers have walked up our brick steps to find fresh, organically grown food and flowers, waiting for them to take home.

The first few weeks of the CSA season, our boxes brim with shades of green—lettuce, arugula, asparagus, maybe some broccoli and snow peas—all things I love to eat. But what I'm really waiting for are the strawberries, those scrumptious berries—juicy, sweet, and ruby-red all the way through, perfect for eating right out of the carton, one-by-one, or sliced and served with a splash of cream.

Years ago, when folks around Durham were just starting to participate in CSAs, I wrote a column about sustainable agriculture for the *Independent Weekly*. My first piece focused on Ken Dawson, who farms Maple Spring Gardens with his wife, Libby Outlaw. I knew him personally and ate his CSA produce week after week, so it seemed only natural to interview him.

I visited him at the farm. It was July, and the fields looked like tapestries. Silky yellow corn tassels fluttered near gold black-eyed Susans that grew next to feathery asparagus ferns. Ken was the first farmer I had ever talked to about farming. Thin and wiry with salt-and-pepper hair, he got into it because he loves to grow things. He started his first organic garden in 1972, and in 1990, he and Libby bought Maple Spring Gardens.

The land was worn out. Years of tobacco farming had so depleted the soil that they didn't find a single earthworm on the property. Ken explained how they brought the earth back to life, building the soil through composting and cover cropping, then rotating crops and planting a variety of produce to promote biodiversity. Today the 61-acre farm supports ninety different kinds of berries, vegetables, and flowers, most of them sold directly to consumers through the CSA or at farmers' markets.

As Ken described the challenges and rewards of running a small organic farm, the conversation turned to strawberries, his voice filling with pride when he told me about his decision to grow them. Many predicted it couldn't be done, that organic strawberries would never grow in this climate.

"Well, for thirty years I've heard you can't do this or you can't do that, and I've made a career of doing it anyway," he told me.

I left our interview with a new appreciation for what it takes to grow food—the time, hard work, and sheer determination required. I think about that conversation every time I eat Ken's strawberries.

The CSA shares come in two sizes: small and regular. A small box usually holds about six different items, and it's the perfect size for my husband, Don, my seven-year-old daughter, Isabel, and me. I must confess we don't always make the best use of the produce. I haven't yet figured out what to do with fennel. And the peppers are beautiful—glossy yellow, red, and green—but often they get sliced, dropped in the freezer, and left to languish behind the frozen corn.

Still, we eat a lot of fresh produce in season because we participate in the CSA. In May I gobble up as many of those strawberries as I can, because I know they'll outshine any I taste during the rest of the year. The same is true for Maple Spring's asparagus and sugar snap peas.

With a box of fresh ingredients to work with each week, I'm more willing to try new recipes. Sure, some are a bust, like the brownish-gray eggplant soup that stayed in our freezer for years. But others, like home-made tomato sauce, vegetable lasagna, and butternut squash soup, become ever-evolving works-in-progress that show up regularly at our dinner table.

We also have a new family tradition thanks to the CSA. One Tuesday every fall, Maple Spring delivers dozens of pumpkins. Too big to fit into the boxes, these gourds are not smooth and round like jack-o'-lanterns, but lumpy and bumpy, each one a slightly different shade of orange. They are perfect for baking, and a few years ago, Don and Isabel started using ours to make pie. Together they scoop out the brightly colored flesh from inside the pumpkin and mix it with cream and spices. Both are proud of this father-daughter creation, which has become a dessert we share with friends during holiday meals.

It's March, and already Isabel is asking when "farm day" will start. For her, these CSA Tuesdays are special events. Come April, the Maple Spring van pulls up just before 4:30 PM, and already people are sitting in cars, waiting for their produce. During the next few hours folks walk, bike, or drive from across Durham to our porch. Adults chat with friends and gather up vegetables and flowers to take home, while kids swing in the front yard. It feels like a party.

Wednesday mornings are occasions, too, because someone always forgets to pick up a box. We tell people that if produce is still on our porch at 8:30 AM, it's ours. Initially this was not our policy, but over the years, we've learned it motivates folks to pick up their food and—more importantly—gives us time to figure out what to do with it before it spoils.

First thing every Wednesday morning, I check the porch to see how many boxes are sitting there. By 8:45 I'm opening them up, pulling out my favorite things to put in the refrigerator. Then, as I'm filling the drawers and shelves, Don reminds me that we cannot possibly consume all this in one week.

And he's right. No matter how tasty that kale or cauliflower looks, we can only eat so much before next Tuesday, when another box of fresh produce will arrive at our doorstep. So we share the bounty. It's not enough for the soup kitchen, but plenty to give neighbors who put up with extra traffic on Tuesdays. Usually Don bags it up and makes the deliveries—something he loves to do—and last year Isabel joined the effort, taking bags next door and across the street before school.

Isabel says she looks forward to farm day because it's fun to have everyone come to our house. Most of the time I agree, though there are days I ask her to pick up our box, while I retreat into the kitchen to avoid the crowd. Overall I appreciate the sense of community the CSA creates. And often, after a dinner of stir-fried vegetables, salad, and sliced tomatoes—all from the farm—I feel a sense of well-being take root in my chest. The simple act of eating this food, which tastes so good and is so good for us, connects us to Ken and Libby, the farm, and our neighbors. Knowing this nourishes my soul as surely as the food fuels my body.

It's this broader connection, to the land and to people who appreciate what it provides, that I think about when I reflect on what the CSA brings to our porch. Last summer, Isabel and I met friends for dinner at Weaver Street Market, where farmer photos hang above the fruit and vegetable displays. When we walked into the produce section, she grabbed my arm with one hand, and pointed up with other.

"Mom! Look Mom! There's farmer Ken. Our farmer."

SIDNEY CRUZE is a freelance writer whose articles have appeared in many publications, including *Our State*, *Wildlife in North Carolina*, and the *Independent Weekly*. She also works as a local food systems consultant with the Center for Environmental Farming Systems at North Carolina State University.

Watching Pictures in the Dark

KIRSTEN MULLEN

AS THE EXPERIENCE OF WATCHING PICTURES in the dark on the big screen with friends who live down the street becomes increasingly rare, I am reminded of one of Durham's bygone treasures—the Center Theater at the Lakewood Shopping Center—and of my time spent in the segregated theaters of my youth. The Center Theater was hardly distinguished by its architecture or decor. What we valued was the communal experience largely shaped by Jim Crow that defined our separate and unequal communities. Even today, the compulsory segregation of the past continues to inform the behavior of white and nonwhite moviegoers.

We moved to Durham in 1983. And in an entry from my 1992 journal, I wrote about Spike Lee's *Malcolm X*, the last film I saw at the Center Theater. The original Center Theater opened in 1938 at the corner of Corcoran and West Chapel Hill streets. Like the five other movie houses architect Erle G. Stilwell of Hendersonville had designed in North Carolina, Center Theater was built for the era of segregation. City boosters were proud of the new building; the *Durham Morning Herald* reported glowingly, if inaccurately, "there has been no discrimination in quality or appointments." *White* patrons enjoyed a "whites-only" mezzanine, lounge, balcony, and large decorative restrooms; *colored* patrons were allowed to watch movies from a "colored balcony" that was behind the whites-only balcony and only accessible by a separate stairway. Unadorned single-stall toilets were constructed for colored customers above the upper-most balcony.

That theater was replaced in 1966 with the new Center Theater, a nondescript hulk of a building, finshed with an electric curlicue of its name displayed above the marquee. Located in the busy Lakewood Shopping Center, it seemed to rise up from a concrete sea. Constructed post-integration and devoid of Jim Crow-era partitioning, the theater signaled a new era in Durham.

For a brief period, as black films with nationwide distribution emerged, both black and white audiences came out to support them. By 1992, however, after the reign of the "blaxploitation" and gangster films of the Seventies and Eighties, many whites (and not a few blacks) had retreated, and the Center became a largely segregated institution. Whites were especially scarce when the director of the featured film was black and beloved, or black and controversial, or if the story was one of black struggle or black liberation—doing battle with "The Man," the ubiquitous though sometimes unnamed or unseen white oppressor—or if the cast included high profile black actors.

Segregated theaters, either de facto or de jure, had been a part of our lives since I could remember. As a child living in Fort Worth, Texas, I often visited my grandparents and would catch the Saturday double-feature at the neighborhood's Grand Theater. It was the 1960s, and the movies brought me joy, terror, expectation, mystification, and emotional connection in equal measure. Safe within our perfect world we would settle into our seats, let the images wash over us, and cheer for our favorite performers. Certain film-going memories, like sitting in a black audience, watching a movie with a prominent black star, stand out. Grand Theater audiences participated in a familiar communal "call and response," not unlike that practiced in many black churches where congregants signal they are following the minister's sermon by verbal affirmation.

At movie houses located in black neighborhoods throughout the South, audience participation was both expected and excitedly anticipated. If you wanted a quiet movie experience where everyone remained seated and no one spoke once the lights were dimmed, you could go to a downtown theater where most of the audience were certain to be white, but you also had to cope with a range of discriminatory treatments that were exemplified by sitting in the "colored" balcony. If, instead, you sought a window into black people's political opinions or were curious about hair, fashion, and sartorial trends, or music featured in a particular film, or if you were inclined to enthusiastically and vocally support your favorite on-screen hero (or denigrate your favorite villain), neighborhood theaters were the place to be.

One frequently screened movie was *The Defiant Ones*, director Stanley Kramer's film about two escaped convicts, joined together at the wrist by a heavy chain, who were on the run in the Deep South. Noah Cullen (Sidney Poitier) had only contempt for white people, and John "Joker" Jackson (Tony Curtis) was equally contemptuous of blacks. The audience, primed for the film, began "talking back" to the screen almost immediately. Different factions ran their own commentaries as the two shackled men attacked each other verbally and with their fists, staved off hunger, coped with inclement weather and rough terrain, and narrowly escaped a lynch mob determined to hang them both. (When Joker pleads, "You can't lynch me. I'm white," someone in the theater yelled, "Well, you're a nigger today!") Finally, the escapees broke free of the manacles. By then Joker was wounded in a shooting and Cullen had evaded the treachery of the Dismal Swamp. The men had become friends.

Toward the end of the movie, when the two men had an opportunity to catch a freight train to freedom before it picked up too much steam, Cullen managed to hop aboard, but Joker, running alongside, was a step too slow. Cullen leaned out precariously to grab Joker's hand and pull him bodily onto the moving train, his face contorted from the effort. When he urged his friend, "Come on, come on. Don't give up," the audience was clearly divided. "Run Joker, run," my sister and I yelled. Others cautioned, "Let him go. Let that cracker go, man. Save yourself," pointedly taking exception to the film director's intended liberal message. If you don't know how the story ends, you can see for yourself. It remains an entertaining and thought-provoking film. Significantly, Poitier's name was featured on the billing alongside that of Curtis, a first for him, and both men were nominated for the Academy Award (the film won Best Cinematography—Black and White, and Best Writing, Story and Screenplay).

There is a wide range of cultural norms around moviegoing. My East Indian friends speak fondly of their tradition of visiting with friends and sharing food brought from home while children play in the aisles during their favorite four-and-a-half-hour-long Bollywood films. Meanwhile, white friends (and not a few black ones) express frustration with people who talk in the movies. Differences in taste and cultural preference, what my sister calls "aesthetic apartheid," help me realize just how difficult it is to have an integrated experience where everyone feels comfortable. So we actively bridge and translate cultural experiences for each other.

Malcolm X brought all these elements together in a nationally released production, which made it a perfect film to see with a majority black audience.

For my family, many of our black friends, and a few of our more adventurous white friends, Center Theater was where we went to luxuriate in a big screen experience and celebrate community. And it was *the* place to tap into or become one with the zeitgeist of black America. While it was never discussed, we understood that our presence was an implicit guarantee of safety for our white guests. When one of them wanted something from the concession stand or needed to visit the restroom, a black member of our party escorted them without comment.

The day *Malcolm X* opened, we organized a large group—seven people—and stood in line to purchase tickets. Matinee idol Denzel Washington was on a roll, after having appeared on television in the medical drama *St. Elsewhere* as heart throb Dr. Philip Chandler, and on the big screen in *Mississippi Masala, Ricochet, Liberators,* and *Glory,* for which he had received a Best Supporting Actor Oscar three years prior. The crowd at the Center Theater was psyched. "I heard Denzel is going to get the Academy Award for Best Actor," the man in line ahead of us said.

Joining in the fun, one of our white friends added, "The new Sidney," referring to Sidney Poitier of *The Defiant Ones* fame. (Two years after making that film, Poitier had become the first black actor to receive the coveted Best Actor Oscar for his role as Homer in *Lilies of the Field* in 1960.)

Two teenage girls standing nearby and their male companion considered his comment. "Denzel's cool like Sidney, but he's got it all over Mr. Tibbs on the pretty tip," one of the girls offered dreamily. That would be Philadelphia Police Lieutenant Virgil Tibbs, the cerebral character Poitier nailed in the 1967 mystery film, *In the Heat of the Night,* that had spawned a television show of the same name that ran from 1988 to 1995.

"Man, I can't believe [Denzel] did a love scene with that [East] Indian woman [Sarita Choudhury, who plays Mina in *Mississippi Masala*]," added her girlfriend. "I mean, if he had been white he could have stipulated in his contract that he didn't have to do it."

"Refuse the love scene?! Are you crazy?" their male companion responded, incredulous. "Did you *see* that woman? I mean, she was fine!" outlining the actor's figure in the air with his hands. "I wish *I* was Denzel."

When a woman a few feet away cracked, "Don't they all!" the entire crowd erupted with laughter. We were already having a good time and the movie had not even started.

As we found our seats, various patrons were issuing shout-outs to their friends: "Yo, Blue Man, Big Time? You in the house?"

"Zeke, that you? Big Time couldn't make it. Where you at?"

Everyone's mood shifted quickly once the movie started and the iconic 1991 footage of Rodney King being beaten mercilessly by the Los Angeles police filled the screen, followed by an image of a gigantic American flag engulfed in flames, the Stars and Stripes reduced to a red, white, and blue *X*.

"Goddam cops gotta pay. That's what I'm talking about!" someone shouted. A resounding chorus of "Yea, they've got to pay," echoed throughout the theater. We settled into a tense silence as the film shifted to World War II-era Boston and Malcolm Little, the flamboyant and reckless hustler whose street ways were unknown to most of the audience.

Denzel Washington's and Angela Bassett's on-screen transformations knocked us out. "Look at those clean zoot suits," one admirer called out. Inspired by the Lindy Hoppers in the Roseland Ballroom scene as the band played Lionel Hampton's "Flying Home," two couples jumped into the aisle, whooped, and spun each other around to the delight of the Center Theater audience.

"Where did Denzel learn to dance like that?" one woman asked.

"My man is rockin' some Malcolm," someone down front affirmed.

"He looks more like Malcolm than Malcolm!" another man shouted.

Angela Bassett played Malcolm X's wife, Betty Shabazz, in minimal makeup, somber colors, and a head covering, and was completely unrecognizable. A graduate of both Yale University and the Yale School of Drama, Bassett by 1992 was a member of a small minority of black female actors who enjoyed steady employment and avoided being typecast. She had played a range of roles, from Fran in the bizarre *Critters 4* and U.S. Attorney Sinclair in the black comedy and graphic horror film *Innocent Blood* (directed by John Landis of *An American Werewolf in London* fame) to *Boyz in the Hood*'s Reva Devereaux-Styles, ex-wife of Furious Styles (Laurence Fishburne) and mother of Tré (Cuba Gooding), whose friends are pulled into gang life with tragic results. Bassett had earned her box office gold status.

Watching *Malcolm X* that day, we cheered when our favorite icons were on-screen—Delroy Lindo played West Indian Archie, and Spike Lee cast himself as Shorty, the thief who schools Malcolm in how to dress and introduces him to the town's fast and cool set. And we thrust our fists in the air during the cameo appearances of Black Panther Party cofounder Bobby Seale, Nelson Mandela, and the Rev. Al Sharpton.

When Denzel's character calls out to his followers to see the world through his eyes, we were right there with him, ready with our response. "You're not an American!" he charges.

"That's right!" the theater rang out.

"We didn't land on Plymouth Rock. Plymouth Rock landed on us!"

"Tell the truth, Brother!" several of us yelled back to the screen.

"You been sitting down, laying down, and bowing down for four hundred years. I think it's time to stand up."

"Preach!"

"You been had, you been took, you been hoodwinked, bamboozled, led astray, run amok."

I think it fair to say that everyone in the theater knew how Malcolm X would die but the horror of the assassination on the screen ripped through the audience. Several people screamed. Many of us cried.

Finally, someone called out, "They had to know who did it. I mean everybody saw. How could they get away with that?"

"Why did he have to die like that?" someone else asked.

At least half the audience stayed to watch the entire credit list—some out of respect for Spike Lee, the cast, and cinema crew, others to see who the musicians and consultants were who had been enlisted to provide authenticity. We stayed up half the night discussing what we had seen, read aloud passages from Alex Haley's *The Autobiography of Malcolm X*, and toasted the power of cinema, border crossing, and community.

Folklorist and arts consultant **KIRSTEN MULLEN** founded *Carolina Circuit Writers,* a literary consortium that brings writers of color to the Carolinas. She is president of the North Carolina Folklife Institute and was a member of the Freelon Adjaye Bond concept development team that was awarded the Smithsonian National Museum of African American History and Culture commission. Her essays have appeared in museum catalogs and in *American Legacy, USA Today, Historic Preservation Magazine, NC Historical Review, Herald-Sun, Independent Weekly, Americana, Texas Observer, Texas Architect,* and *Black Enterprise.*

Where Durham Works Out

DIANE DANIEL

I NEEDED A PLACE TO TAKE YOGA. It was early 2004, my fourth month in Durham, and I was still feeling my way around. I liked what I saw in my new hometown: a rich stew of folks from different races, incomes, education levels, and backgrounds in a city small enough that I was already bumping into acquaintances.

My partner and I had moved down from Boston for her job, but I wasn't a stranger to the area. Raleigh was home until I was sixteen, and Durham was where Granny Fanny lived. At least once a month, Mom and Dad, with me in the backseat whining about my dad's pipe smoke, would make the drive up Highway 70 for Sunday dinner at Granny's. Sometimes in the summer I'd stay with her on weekends. Granny would let me watch TV past my bedtime and spoiled me with unlimited bottles of Coca-Cola and Krispy Kreme doughnuts warmed in the toaster oven, then slathered with peanut butter. One of the only things she wouldn't let me do, despite my pleas, was swim in the public pool. "You're not going in the water with those woolly-hairs," said Granny, issuing an edict different from any I'd heard at home. Even now, forty-five years later, I can still see Granny scowling at the thought of her granddaughter swimming with black people.

After asking my new friends and neighbors for yoga referrals, I chose a private studio. The teacher, a willowy former ballerina, wore a tight bun and shared strong opinions about alignment. We students were white, middle-class professional women in our forties. The discussions often veered to education, especially finding alternatives to Durham public middle schools, and everyone shared news they'd read in the *New York Times*, but not the *Herald-Sun* or *News & Observer*. My fellow yogis were nice enough, but they didn't seem invested in Durham the way I'd started to feel.

When the instructor announced she was leaving and the class wouldn't continue, I wasn't all that disappointed. I recalled that our realtor had mentioned a YMCA downtown, just a few miles from home. I stopped by late in the afternoon to pick up a schedule, which included yoga, and take a look around. A black woman in her forties was leading an aerobics class filled with black and white women of all shapes and ages. In the expansive fitness area, seniors cycled next to twenty-somethings, an instructor assisted a man in a wheelchair, and young men lifted dumbbells while watching their biceps ripple in the mirror.

Durham was here, working out. I signed up on the spot.

Now, years later, the Y is still one of the few places I frequent that reflects my city's population. Not only do we comprise all skin colors, we're gay and straight, PhDs and GEDs, Christians and nonbelievers, wealthy and low-income (the Y gives financial assistance). I appreciate all the differences, but especially the racial diversity, because in my life it's rare. Part of my lack of exposure is due to working at home and not having children, so I'm more isolated. But that's not the whole story. Like in many heterogeneous populations, we self-segregate, sometimes because of interests, sometimes not. Even my historically black neighborhood of Walltown tends to favor one color over another block by block.

It's different at the Y (although admittedly yoga draws a largely Caucasian crowd). At muscle pump, we grimace side by side as Anthony leads us

84

through killer abdominal crunches on Saturday mornings. In Sue's spinning class, we yell out our names and welcome fellow cyclists during rollicking introductions. And, yes, we splash in the same water in the pool. I'd like to think Granny Fanny would be okay with that by now.

I think many of us—black and white—crave opportunities to interact in settings like these, where we're just doing our thing, naturally. We don't usually acknowledge this openly, which is why I so appreciated one instructor's comment at the start of an aerobics class held on Martin Luther King Jr. weekend in 2011.

"Let's dedicate this class to Dr. King," she said. "Without him, we might not be here together." We students nodded silently but didn't make eye contact. I wanted to shout, "Amen!" I thanked the instructor after class, not only for the sentiment but for expressing it.

Several years ago, the Y opened a smaller, spiffier branch at the American Tobacco Campus, which is home mostly to offices.

On my first visit there, I spotted no youngsters and no people of color, except for the front desk staff.

"Can you believe this new Y? I love it here," gushed a woman in the quiet locker room after class. "You don't feel like you're in Durham."

"Funny, that's exactly what I don't like about it," I said, smiling back.

I do take some classes at American Tobacco, but I much prefer the downtown location. My favorite day is Saturday, when the mornings feel like a joyous meet-up on the town green. Parents arrive with their children, friends connect, teens congregate.

I admit, though, sometimes I can take only so much "community." In February and March, for instance, my Saturday group exercise class, held in the gym, gets overtaken by families lining the walls to wait for the start of kiddie basketball. But then I watch youngsters toting balls half the size of their bodies and my heart softens.

As it is with any family, I've had some serious issues with the Y. The year I joined, a brouhaha broke out when Duke University, Durham's largest employer, and the Y ended an agreement to waive initiation fees for Duke employees because the Y, under the leadership of its parent YMCA of the Triangle, sadly wouldn't offer family discounts to same-sex couples. Ultimately, the Y found a way out of the mess by abolishing all discounts for couples. I hope they'll one day bring them back—for all partners.

In 2007, the Triangle group announced more harsh news, that it would close the YMCA Lakewood branch, a community gathering place for forty years. Members fought back hard, forming the Committee to Save the Lakewood YMCA. Their impassioned pleas, published in a *Herald-Sun* column, echoed my sentiments about the downtown location: "The Lakewood Y has been a home to adults and children, black and white, rich and poor. . . . This sharing of facilities by a broad range of our population is what the YMCA is all about." Thanks to the group's Herculean efforts, a renovated Lakewood Y opened in 2012 under a partnership formed with Durham County and the Durham Public Schools.

No doubt, more Y dramas will surface, but for now, all is calm.

One day, as I was writing this, I toured the downtown Y with a critical eye, making sure it was really everything I'd said it was. As I walked into the lobby, I saw a woman with a girl who looked to be her daughter, both wearing traditional Islamic abaya dresses and head scarves. I smiled at the timing.

I still take yoga, about twice a week. When people ask what kind I practice, they expect me to answer with some official variety such as hatha, ashtanga, or vinyasa.

"I do the Y version," I always answer. "It's a mix of all types, just the way I like it."

DIANE DANIEL writes about travel, sustainable agriculture, the environment, artists, and activists. She is the author of the guidebook *Farm Fresh North Carolina* and her work has appeared in publications including the *New York Times, Boston Globe, Washington Post, News & Observer, Budget Travel, Southern Living,* and *Our State.*

Durham, Unvarnished

DAWN BAUMGARTNER VAUGHAN

DURHAM COUNTY JAIL and the Durham Performing Arts Center stand right next to each other downtown. It's very Durham. The Bull City, you see, doesn't give, or take, any bull. It doesn't hide from itself. And so, when the Durham Performing Arts Center (DPAC) was constructed next to the jail, it was met with comments like, "Well, that's Durham." The jail is a decent looking building, as jails go. Visitors to DPAC sometimes ask what the neighboring building is and are surprised by the answer.

It's just Durham, unvarnished.

There are fancy neighborhoods and there are busted neighborhoods, but a lot of the city is a middle class mix, and on the outskirts of downtown you'll find a souped-up Victorian house next to a boarded-up one. While some churches moved to the suburbs, others embraced their downtown location when the city center was far from today's revitalization. St. Philip's Episcopal Church is near a homeless shelter and public housing. Rather than putting up a fence, they planted a community garden.

When I started as a reporter at the *Herald-Sun* in early 2006, I was struck most by Durham's ability to tell it like it is.

One of my favorite quotes in a religion story I wrote was from Evangelist Alice Bailey-McKinnis, who started a ministry at one of the most crime-ridden, poverty-stricken intersections in Northeast Central Durham.

"Why are we sitting in the church witnessing to other witnesses?" Bailey-McKinnis told me in 2009. "That's so boring. We just witness to each other, jump up and down and go home and eat some mashed potatoes. This is where the party is." She worked for change from within, not outside.

Calling people out is some of what Durham does best.

Like Barry Johnson, who lives at the end of the Bryant Pedestrian Bridge. You know the one, the lighted blue arc you drive under on the Durham Freeway. It crosses two sides of a broken neighborhood, two sides of boarded-up houses and residents who have had enough. That's who Barry Johnson is, a man who has had enough. I met him on a day when volunteers from the city's Neighborhood Improvement Services and Environmental Protection Agency were sprucing up an empty lot near his home. He considered the sprucing just bread and circus, a show that wouldn't fix anything, especially the folks running across the bridge at night to try breaking into his house. So Johnson shoos them off, back to the side that garners more police patrols, he said.

My first week of work at the *Herald-Sun*, there was a shooting on a city bus in front of the downtown library. First impressions of Durham are often wrong. I didn't know Durham then. Now, when I think of a DATA bus, I don't think of the rare shooting, but of a love story.

Romania Garner and Quincey Myers met on the city bus. I went to their wedding, a joyful and unpretentious affair with a bride so assured and calm that she sewed up the back of a bridesmaid's dress moments before going down the aisle. The modern-day *Brady Bunch* couple (she has four children, he has two) is the real deal.

They would have never met if they hadn't taken the #4 DATA bus from downtown Durham on a June evening in 2010. Their romance was like a fairy tale or an old movie, but a real one. It doesn't get more real than having to take three buses to get to work. On that fateful summer night, Garner was on the second of three routes she took home to northern Durham from the salon at the Brier Creek Walmart. As she boarded the #4 downtown, she saw a handsome man in a pressed shirt and dreadlocks. She asked who did his hair and gave him her business card.

Quincey Myers took the card, gave Garner his number, and spent the ride checking basketball scores on his phone. But Garner, who never talks to anyone on the bus—much less asks a man out—decided to send a text. She typed that he didn't have to wait to get his hair done to give her a call.

"I had to smile," Myers told me a few days before their wedding. He was sitting at the front of the bus and she was several seats behind him. "I turned around and she looked out the window," he said. When they got to the next stop, Myers asked if he could walk her home. He's from New York City, so he's a walker, he said, but Garner said she had another bus to take the last few miles. Myers asked her to wait for the next bus, coming by his place instead. She said yes. He was cordial. They talked about their lives and their children. Then he walked her back to the bus stop. She started to get on the bus, then stepped off again and kissed him—their first kiss.

"When she came back down the stairs, it was like a movie. I could hear the theme music. I couldn't have made it up," he said.

Myers proposed the following spring, and quickly bought a drugstore engagement ring. She wore it until it turned green. She told him she didn't care about a fancy ring, she just wanted his last name.

"I don't have a problem riding the bus, and she doesn't either," he said. Garner told DATA about their love found on a bus, and Triangle Transit congratulated the couple with a card and two 31-day bus passes as a wedding gift.

The groom's mother said it's funny how you meet someone when you least expect it. She met her husband on the New York City train.

Couples like Romania and Quincey are what make my job worthwhile, sharing their life stories with the rest of Durham through the local newspaper.

Often I'll interview an old-timer who worked for the paper in its previous entities, the *Durham Morning Herald* and the *Durham Sun.* Like Bryan Turner, who once worked in circulation, then spent a career selling vacuum cleaners. Long retired, he still carried vacuum replacement parts in his trunk in case an old customer needed them. Turner moved to Durham for his job, but he's like a lot of other older guys who served in World War II, married and raised families here: Men now in their eighties who graduated from the old Durham High School in the 1940s when gym class involved the same kinds of drills they'd face in basic training before going to war. Those who came back married their high school sweethearts and got back to the business of living, working, and raising families in Durham. They were factory workers and insurance agents, doctors, and salesmen.

Durham is Bobby Lougee, the once-a-Marine-always-a-Marine who knows all those old friends from Durham High going on seventy years now. Lougee has spent years organizing their class reunions, though some alumni see each other regularly anyway. At least one group of men from the Class of 1944 have been friends forever, meeting monthly for lunch for over half a century since their school cafeteria days. I joined them one day a few years ago to interview them for a story, and they joked around with each other like the kids they once were. This is who Durham really is, I thought.

Often the most interesting stories come from those behind the scenes. I've covered the big names who speak from the pulpit of Duke University Chapel, but the best interview came from the man who told me about the little mouse carved into the wood next to the imposing organ pipes. Oscar Dantzler, the custodian of Duke Chapel, is the man with the keys to everything, including the elevator to the top of the Gothic cathedral. He took a photographer and me up there one day when I was writing about his appearance in a documentary about ivory tower custodians. I got a spectacular view of Durham — and on the clear day, Chapel Hill and Raleigh, too — that only Oscar Dantzler could provide. He likes to show people cool things, like the view from the top of the chapel and that church mouse. He also loves to fish, and on his days off goes fishing at dawn. He doesn't eat the fish, though. After growing up eating it for breakfast, lunch, and dinner, he's had his fill. I love that a dedicated fisherman doesn't eat the fish — just enjoys the time spent fishing.

The people I meet in Durham are what make the city what it is, though I love the brick tobacco and textile factories repurposed for new business. When I look at those historic buildings, I picture what it was like working there, and I've met those who know. The Durham Performing Arts Center is next to the American Tobacco Campus — former factories and now thriving office space, restaurants, and a place for music on the lawn under the Lucky Strike Tower, which is lit up each Christmas. New Durham gathers to play where Old Durham once worked. At DPAC, I cover the Broadway shows that come to town. I review the performances, but I also interview beforehand the people that make it all come together. I've talked to union electricians and Tony Award-winning stars and seen the talent and hard work it takes to succeed. As much fun as it is to be in the audience, I like knowing what goes on before the curtain goes up. It's about seeing the whole picture — sweat, struggle, triumph, and reward. Just like Durham itself.

DAWN BAUMGARTNER VAUGHAN has been a features reporter at the *Herald-Sun* since 2006. She has received two North Carolina Press Association awards for criticism. She previously worked at three Virginia newspapers before coming to the Piedmont. Portions of this essay first appeared in the *Herald-Sun*.

Views from Before

Remembering a Town Father

JEAN BRADLEY ANDERSON

NEW TOWNS ATTRACT MEN with ambition and willingness to take risks. Such men also commonly possess courage, self-reliance, and optimism. If a pioneer can sell himself and his services as well, he will certainly reap the rewards and may gain the esteem of his community. Doctor Claiborne Parrish fitted the mold, but his gallantry and integrity set him apart.

He was born 28 May 1807 in then Orange County, North Carolina, long before the county and town of Durham existed. The son of Edith and Allen Parrish, he grew up in the Flat River area called Round Hill, now Bahama, where his grandfather Ansel, or Hansel, Parrish had received a land grant in 1780. He came of sturdy stock; his father lived to ninety and his mother to eighty-seven. The given name *Doctor* was often reserved for a seventh son of a seventh son, who was believed to possess the powers of healing; however, only three of his brothers are accounted for: James, Nelson, and Isham. But D.C. Parrish had powers of a different sort; he was a born leader with a common touch.

He burst onto the stage of history in 1835 described in a neighbor's letter to U.S. Senator Willie P. Mangum, relating the news of the community to the man they all knew as Judge Mangum.

> There is no news among us Judge that is worth relating. I suppose it wouldn't be much out of place to tell you of a sale scene at Ginny Taylor's de'd [deceased] last Tuesday yesterday was a week. Those contrary republicans and devlish clan that you have around you when at home; the Boullings, Dukes, & Carringtons, formed a sort of Jackson club and possessed themselves of his leading principle, war & bloodshed. They commenced their work upon our humble wagon-maker but true whig Haywood Gooch and there was not a man on the ground but was afraid to go to his relief but our noble spirited Col. D.C. Parrish, who rushed in at the risk of his own life and succeeded in rescuing him by taking the wolves on his own back. They had Dr under their feet for ten minutes or more endeavoring to beat and stamp him to death and his cowardly friends, strong enough and a plenty of them, was afraid to interfere till at length some disinterested persons, incensed with such outdacious conduct, rushed in, overpowered them, and saved Parrish.

A picture of Parrish from later life shows a man of broad shoulders and square head with an open, animated, even amused look on his face, traits which tell of mental as well as physical vigor, just the sort who, with humor and high spirits, might have jumped into a fray as much for the fun as for the defense of a friend. He was also tall and muscular.

Parrish earned the title "colonel" in the local militia, Forty-seventh, or Hillsborough Regiment. Militia titles were elective offices at that time and won very much as popularity contests. He also became a justice of the peace, in 1839, entitling him to be called *squire* (for *esquire*); but what Southerner worth his salt would choose *squire* over *colonel*? D.C. Parrish was always Colonel.

The census records through 1860 consistently listed Parrish as a farmer, but farming did not really suit him. It was too solitary an occupation. Running a store, first at Round Hill, later at South Lowell, and finally at Durham, better answered his convivial bent. His store also supplied black-smithing and shoemaking, probably skills of Parrish slaves. In the 1840s, the federal government chose his Round Hill store for a post office, and Parrish was made postmaster.

His interests were many. In 1841 he got religion. At Moore's Chapel in Granville County he experienced the epiphany every ardent Method-ist longed for: one overwhelming instant of awareness and conviction of a divine presence. Along with social networks of support and comfort that Methodist churches of nineteenth-century rural America provided, they also added emotional and dramatic coloration to laborious, hum-drum lives. In addition, church membership conferred respectability and standing in the community. Parrish became committed to the church and a "professor of religion," as the phrase was. His experience changed the exu-berant, energetic, young gallant into a responsible leader of the community. The next year at the age of thirty-five, he married Ruth A. Ward, daugh-ter of an Onslow County planter, Benjamin Ward. Parrish had probably met her when she and her sister and brother attended boarding schools in Hillsborough, the nearest town with such amenities. All three young Wards married into local families.

The need for schools closer to home became crucial for Parrish in the late 1840s. By 1850 he had five children, the first already seven years old. Therefore in 1849, he was one of the committee that established a boys' academy at South Lowell, and the next year he alone set up the Round Hill Female Academy. The 1850 census listed, along with five children in his family, a teacher with the apt name of Patty Duty. Par-rish's son, James Edward, seven years old that year, was entrusted to South Lowell and his daughters to Miss Duty. His school problem was solved.

In addition to Parrish's support of religion and education, he actively engaged in politics, a subject that aroused intense partisan heat and hard feelings, as the melee described above attests. Though a Whig from the party's founding in 1834, Parrish was first officially affiliated with it as a representative of Orange County to the Baltimore Convention in 1840. In 1848 he was president of the Rough and Ready Club, organized on behalf of Zachary Taylor's campaign for the U.S. presidency, and in 1850 Parrish only narrowly lost election to the North Carolina General Assembly.

If the plantation, the store, the post office, the school, the church, and the party did not completely engage his energies, Parrish could turn his attention to the Round Hill Debating Society or the Round Hill Temperance Society, of both of which he was secretary. With so much to do, he could be forgiven occasional absentmindedness. In 1849 he advertised the loss of a bundle of papers on the road between Hillsborough and his home; and in 1852 he lost his pocketbook either in Hillsborough or on the road from there to South Lowell. The latter contained $154 in cash and $1,100 in notes, not small amounts to have had in hand in those days. In view of these mishaps his next move was a wise one; in 1854 he was one of a group interested in establishing a local bank.

The record is silent concerning the next twelve years. They were unquestionably busy. Since he owned twelve slaves he had help with the plantation and store. Two more children were added to the family: a boy, who died young when he was kicked in the stomach by a horse, and a fifth little girl. About this time Col. Parrish must have begun to think about the new railroad running across the county and what was happening miles away around the little station called Durham's: Parrish became the owner of a tract of land known as Durham's Station, which he had probably acquired at the estate sale of Bartlett Durham in 1859, and which Parrish advertised for sale in 1860. Certain acreage within the tract had already been sold to others. Among these was, of course, the land conveyed to the railroad and another small tract sold as a place of worship to the Methodist Episcopal Church (later Trinity Methodist Church).

The Civil War interrupted the growth of the burgeoning village around the station. By 1869, however, Parrish had already moved to the newly incorporated village called Durham, and he and his best friend, the Rev. John A. McMannen, were appointed Durham's first tax collectors.

Once free of the financial and emotional drains of war, the little village began to grow at a furious pace, and tobacco factories sprang up like weeds from the bare earth along the tracks. Taverns abounded, maintaining the reputation of "a roaring old place" that the pre-war village had already earned. Crude shops, wooden shanties, and modest shelters, which in the 1850s had hurriedly been set up on muddy lanes with names like Hen-Pec Row and Shake-a-Rag, were soon outgrown, and in the late 1870s newly prosperous men began to erect bigger, better structures and finer houses with exuberant architectural excrescences more reflective of their new wealth. D.C. Parrish had built a small house on Dillard Street, but in 1876 his son, Edward James Parrish, a flamboyant man, could afford to build an opulent, high Victorian mansion at the corner of Dillard and Main. The next year, D.C. Parrish went into business; "Col. D.C. Parrish is now prepared to furnish you boots and shoes at remarkably low figures," his advertisement announced. That year, too, he was elected to the first of his seven terms as mayor of Durham.

As in his prime, Parrish never had too much to do. He belonged to Trinity Methodist Church and the Masonic Lodge, ran his shop, and took on the duties of magistrate. The gallantry that had characterized the young man never deserted him. *The Tobacco Plant* recorded that "a countryman was arraigned before Mayor Parrish last week for using obscene language in the presence of ladies. Col. Parrish is a great ladies' man, and is always ready to come to their rescue. He fined the fellow $12.50 and told him to go his way and sin no more."

Col. Parrish's later years must have been satisfying ones; always popular, he had become venerated and loved as a townsman. By the 1870s other Flat River folk such as the Mangums and Carringtons as well as the Ellerbee Creek Dukes had moved to town. The tobacco manufacturers were elbowing each other for position. There was no shortage of business opportunities, and those who came early caught the upward draft and profited. Parrish saw his son, who started out as an auctioneer and soon built a vast warehouse that could shelter a hundred horses and wagons in its sheds, firmly established in the town economy, and his daughters married to successful men. Two of them married the brothers Julian Shakespeare Carr and Dr. Albert C. Carr. Julian Carr's success in tobacco and cotton manufactory, like the Dukes, brought him great wealth, the display of which culminated in 1886 in his building his mansion "Somerset," the largest and most sumptuous house in town. Two other Parrish daughters married tobacco pioneers, Fielding Lewis and John S. Lockhart.

Col. Parrish must have felt he had made the right move; he had glimpsed the opportunity and seized it. He had risked leaving the plantation, his ancestral acres and community, to test the waters in a raw, new town. Through the years with high principles and gallantry, he had worked to earn a place for himself and family and the respect of his fellow townsmen.

An early historian of Durham, Hiram Paul, wrote of him, "Colonel Parrish was in the highest sense a type of old school Southern Chivalry and hospitality. He was the soul of honour, of courtly and unobtrusive dignity, of lofty bearing, suave manners, tender sympathies and sublime humility; discreet and prudent, yet always candid."

When Col. Parrish died suddenly in 1883 while serving his seventh term as Durham mayor, attended by his son-in-law and surrounded by his family, the town experienced one of its first moments of ceremonial awareness and sobriety. For a short time everything stopped and everyone had time to observe and reflect that with Parrish's death something else had ended—the first chapter of the town's history.

Paul described the memorable day:

> The funeral was held from Trinity M.E. Church, conducted by the Revs. T.A. Boone and J.J. Renn. Long before the hour for services the church was filled to utmost capacity. At fifteen minutes to 4 o'clock p.m., the funeral procession moved off from the residence of Capt. E.J. Parrish, the following gentlemen acting as pall-bearers: James

Southgate, Washington Duke, William Lipscomb, T.L. Peay, W.W. Fuller, Rev. A. Walter, H.A. Reams, Caleb B. Green, W.L. Wall, W.H. Rogers, S.F. Tomlinson, and Robert F. Webb. . . . During the funeral services every business house in town was closed, and the procession of carriages was three-quarters of a mile long. No man has ever lived among us who so entwined the affections of the people around him as did Col. Parrish. He was a friend to everybody and everybody was his friend . . . .

A Town Father was carried to his grave.

JEAN BRADLEY ANDERSON is an historian and author of *Durham County: A History of Durham County, North Carolina; Piedmont Plantation: The Bennehan-Cameron Family and Lands in North Carolina; The Kirklands of Ayr Mount;* and *Carolinian on the Hudson.*

The Sloping Hills

Excerpts from *I Walked the Sloping Hills: A Memoir*

WALTER MATTHEW BROWN

FUNNY, I WAS NEVER AWARE THAT I was being evaluated for performance in "physical culture" . . . at Lyon Park Elementary School, where I was a pupil from 1933 through 1938. Funny, in writing my memoir I took note of this many years later while reviewing my school records. Funnier still: According to Wikipedia, *physical culture* emanated from the Industrial Revolution, as "a perception that members of the middle classes were suffering from various 'diseases of affluence' that were partially attributed to their increasingly sedentary lifestyles." Can you imagine? "Diseases of affluence" on Durham's West End in the 1930s, with every indicator of low-socioeconomic-status neighborhoods?

Lyon Park was—or had been—a Rosenwald school, one of several thousand black schools in the American South, public or private, subsidized with charity grants from the Rosenwald Fund. What greater blessing could a concerned African American mother on Jackson Street in Durham, North Carolina, want for her children! The fund recalls the contributions of Julius Rosenwald, a Jewish philanthropist who was a friend of the educator Booker T. Washington and an adherent of Washington's views on education and self-sufficiency for black Americans.

Mama was successful in persuading school principal G.A. Edwards to enroll me in school earlier than I was legally entitled (or required) to. For one thing, she believed it was a way of insulating me from malevolent influences of the street. But perhaps of greater significance was her conviction that educated people had every advantage over people who were uneducated, and she therefore wanted me to step on the first rung of formal education as soon as possible.

We had a school pep song that went in part, "Lyon Park, we love you best of all. Lyon Park, we'll never let you fall. . . ." And for the most part, I loved my elementary school "best of all." Three Lyon Park school teachers stand out as having the greatest influence in my early education: Misses Nettie Brown, Mary L. Stephens, and Pauline F. Dame.

Nettie Brown wore pretty clothes; she was attractive, kind, and a good teacher. I cannot recall how it came about, but I rode to school daily with her when I was in the second grade, and I walked home from school in the afternoon. I loved Miss Nettie Brown as much as a six-year-old could love a woman four times his age. When I learned in 1934 that she had married a man named Robert "Bob" Clay, I was wounded.

About twenty years later, I was saddened to learn that Mrs. Brown-Clay had developed a severe mental illness. The symptoms were not unlike what I would later come to know as advanced dementia. She was unkempt and obese, and she had an insensate expression as she walked the city streets. Perhaps the thing that kept me from losing my equilibrium whenever I saw her was that she always greeted me with a smile and said something that I construed to be pleasant, though mostly incomprehensible. I loved her still, a love based on my memory of my second-grade teacher who had made a lasting impression on a six-year-old boy.

If there was any laughter in Miss Mary Louise Stephens's third-grade classroom, I don't remember it. It isn't that Miss Stephens was mean or intimidating. She just went about the business of teaching, and she was all business. In Miss Stephens's third grade, "writing" meant penmanship. The only subject for which I received grades below B were the Cs I earned in her writing class. I simply didn't fare well at replicating the hallowed Palmer hand. Could this have been a subconscious incentive when I began to study calligraphic writing thirty years later?

Miss Stephens was a talented pianist, and she used her talent playing for school assemblies and directing dramatic productions that featured her students. One such production was our class's appearance on the campus of North Carolina College for Negroes. Although I don't recall what the occasion was, I have a mental picture of being one in a line of maybe ten or twelve students, each of whom held a placard with a single letter. Together the letters spelled a word, something noble, no doubt. Mine was the letter C, and when it came my turn, I took a step forward and said, "C is for cleanliness. Cleanliness is next to godliness," and stepped back in line. That is all I remember, but nothing has changed: Cleanliness is *still* next to godliness.

A performance I do remember was a Saint Patrick's Day playlet in 1936. In this all-black school . . . we sang "Did Your Mother Come From Ireland?" With hoisted cardboard shamrocks, boys were telling classmate lassies that something in them Irish stole their hearts away. I don't remember that there was a commentary or discussion about diversity in art forms or cross-cultural emphases when we learned the song. Our teacher introduced it to us. We liked the lyrics and the melody. In other words, it was no big deal.

Miss Stephens was also director of the senior choir at my family church, West Durham Baptist Church. Whenever I compare its choral music with that of most other churches . . . I am pleased. It was a precursor to the music I would later sing in high school, in college, and in churches where my wife, our daughters, and I [attended].

. . . "And seeing the multitudes, he went up into a mountain; and when he was set, his disciples came unto him. And he opened his mouth and taught them, saying . . ." Thus begin the Beatitudes from the Sermon on the Mount (Matthew 5:1–15), in which Miss Pauline Fitzgerald Dame, my fourth-grade teacher, led the class in recitation at the beginning of each school day.

The recitation preceded lessons in any of the ten subjects in our fourth-grade curriculum: Reading, Language, Spelling, Geography, History, Arithmetic, Writing, Drawing, Music, and Hygiene. I don't recall that Miss Dame referred to the Sermon at any time other than during the devotional period. Nor do I recall any sermons about the Sermon. It was a ritual, presumably one intended to make us better children, and better adults as well. It must have worked, at least in the school year 1935–1936. I don't remember that Miss Dame had to contend with any major disciplinary problems.

I was delighted when I learned some fifteen years after I was Miss Dame's pupil that her niece was Pauli Murray, the celebrated writer, lawyer, and civil rights activist, and the first African American woman Episcopal priest. The Reverend Dr. Murray may be best known for her book, *Proud Shoes: The Story of an American Family*. A *New York Herald Tribune* reviewer wrote that the book is "of such variety of incidents and such depths and changes of tone as to astonish one who mistakes it simply for a family chronicle." Pauli Murray dedicated *Proud Shoes* "To Caroline, Edmund, Marie, and the memory of Pauline Fitzgerald Dame." In Durham, the Dames lived in a two-story house at 906 Carroll Street. In 2009, the house is still standing.

Miss Dame was in her late forties by the time I reached the fourth grade. She was gentle, of very fair complexion, and had white hair. Parents were fond of her, perhaps because of her matronly demeanor and her demonstrably keen interest in their children. I believe she prepared me well for the fifth grade and quite likely beyond.

———————————

Durham, North Carolina, in my school days was a typical city of racial apartheid in the American South. Caste systems in both races were a stark reality. In my years as a student at Hillside High School, I got to know well many of my fellow students from every section of Durham. I observed that students who lived in the southern section of Durham were presumed by some teachers to be academically talented until they proved otherwise. To the contrary, students from other sections of the city were generally presumed by those same teachers to have little academic talent or potential unless *they* proved otherwise.

At that time, the preponderance of black-owned enterprises and the families connected with them lived in the southern part of the city. There were middle-class blacks in other sections . . . but even they looked to southern Durham for opportunities in business, education, and some cultural features that were not available to them in their own communities, and certainly not in white Durham. Black-owned businesses in the West End during the same time were a small grocery store, barbershops and beauty salons, a photography studio, and an ice cream store. There was also a pool hall where I saw only black faces. . . .

According to R. Kelly Bryant, longtime official with the Durham Business and Professional Chain (the black counterpart to the city's chamber of commerce), the categories of black enterprises in southern Durham during the 1940s included

> Hillside High School
>
> Stanford L. Warren branch of the Durham Public Library
>
> Lincoln Hospital
>
> *Carolina Times,* a weekly newspaper
>
> North Carolina College for Negroes
>
> Regal Theatre
>
> Biltmore Hotel
>
> Garrett's Drug Store
>
> United Service Organization (USO)
>
> The city's largest black churches: White Rock Baptist Church, St. Joseph's AME Church, and St. Mark AME Zion Church (there were, of course, other churches in southern Durham but the only criterion I use here is size of membership)

North Carolina Mutual Life Insurance Company and Mechanics and Farmers Bank, on Parrish Street in downtown Durham (some offices of lawyers and physicians were also there)

Offices of the Durham Committee on Negro Affairs (later renamed the Committee on the Affairs of Black People)

At times, since the passing of laws requiring the desegregation of public schools in America, I have heard generalizations by some black brothers and sisters—mostly sisters for some reason—that black teachers of generations past were good and compassionate. More often than not, there was either an explicit statement or an implication that black teachers were inherently more compassionate than white teachers.

I never had a white teacher in elementary school or high school. So I could not say from direct personal experience whether white teachers during my era were characteristically good, bad, or somewhere in between. I can say that my teachers at Lyon Park Elementary School were mostly good. But I have always believed that a few of my high school teachers were so mean-spirited that they were the prime reason that some students dropped out of school.

I have been haunted with memories of instances in which some Hillside teachers verbally abused students among those from the not-so-fortunate sections of the city. A case in point was Mr. KJP.

Pearlena B. attended the East End Elementary School before she entered the seventh grade at Hillside. We were classmates in Mr. KJP's eighth-grade civics class. Pearlena was attractive, well groomed, and soft-spoken, and she was as good a student as most of us. Once when Pearlena did not know the textbook answer to a question asked by Mr. KJP, he described her to the class as "beautiful but dumb."

Pearlena survived Mr. KJP. We were in the same graduating class. But she has never attended a high school class reunion. . . . I would not have singled out this case except that others who graduated from Hillside during the same era have shared with me equally reprehensible stories about the same teacher.

The most disquieting note is that Pearlena was not only the victim of racial apartheid; she also was the victim of class apartheid enforced by a black teacher in the only high school she could attend because of her race. In the June 3, 2002, issue of the *New Yorker,* Stephen L. Carter (Professor of Law at Yale University and author of the 1991 book *Reflections of an Affirmative Action Baby*) is quoted by interviewer David Owen: "There are plenty of Black kids who look out at the world and see a place that has no room for them." I maintain that tragedy is heaped upon tragedy when black children do not see a respectable place for them in either the white *or* black world. Who knows how many Pearlenas have been victimized by KJPs who themselves were misfits in a profession that purports to help children develop to their full potential.

Teaching as a profession had far fewer admissions barriers to African Americans, especially in the Southern states, than other professions, including the whole range of human services. It was one of the peculiar byproducts of racial segregation and discrimination. Another byproduct, however, was that an untold number of African Americans pursued teaching as a career when they were far better suited for professions that denied admission to them because of the color of their skin. This problem was gravest when such teachers were hostile, oppressive, or bitter as a consequence of injustices over which their students had absolutely no control. Fortunately for some students, [exemplary teachers like James Schooler Sr.] enabled them to overcome some barriers of legal segregation and discrimination based on social class, or on *perceived* social class. But alas, too many were unable to overcome these odds.

———

As a small boy in Durham's West End, I overheard people refer to North Carolina College for Negroes as *NC State,* and at times simply as *State.*

Some referred to it in those terms when they encouraged me to stay in school "and go on to State" after high school. I had absolutely no idea then that a white land-grant college had been founded in 1887 as North Carolina State College (now North Carolina State University) and was referred to by the general populace as *NC State* and *State*.

I was hardly a youthful visionary, if preparation for attending college is an indicator. I loved school from the first grade on. Not until my senior year in high school, however, did I begin to think seriously about what I would do after graduation. North Carolina College for Negroes (NCC) in my hometown appeared to be the logical next step for me. By that time, I knew I would *not* be going to NC State College in Raleigh.

Two years after I entered NCC, my brother William enrolled in the state's land-grant college for Negroes, North Carolina Agricultural and Technical College in Greensboro (later to become North Carolina A&T State University). It was founded in 1899, twelve years after its white counterpart in Raleigh.

When I entered NCC in September 1943, the institution had a single governing body, its board of trustees. The lone African American on the board was C.C. Spaulding, then president of North Carolina Mutual Life Insurance Company in Durham. Boards of trustees for all state-supported colleges in North Carolina became subordinate to the University of North Carolina Board of Governors when it was established in 1972.

In 1943, the academic year at NCC was divided into quarters instead of semesters. Tuition was $25 per quarter. (The Consumer Price Equivalent [CPE] of this amount in 2009 was $308.09). With additional fees for the first or entrance quarter only—registration, athletic, library and concert, and medical—the "total amount due at entrance" for nonboarding students was $46 (2009 CPE = $566.89). Otherwise, for the second and third quarters, tuition costs were the only costs. For boarding students, the entrance-quarter fee was $121.75 (2009 CPE = $1,500.41). I was a nonboarding student....

Individuals who are uninformed or have distorted information about Southern American history might wonder how one could be awed by a little college in Durham, North Carolina, in the same town as nationally renowned Duke University. It is not so difficult for me to understand. I grew up in the shadow of Duke University, but in my boyhood and adolescent years, there were two different worlds, separate and unequal. These *worlds* retained separate identities even as their constituencies sometimes interacted in sundry ways, generally between the privileged and underprivileged, and too often between the powerful and the powerless. I attended public elementary and high schools in this city and, like my peers, viewed my new school, which happened to be named North Carolina College for Negroes, as an opportunity that was the best that could be provided in my separate and unequal world.

110

Is there any wonder, therefore, that I was favorably impressed with NCC's Administration Building, which included [the offices of founder and president] Dr. [James E.] Shepard, the registrar, bursar, and various personnel deans; an assembly hall and post office; and classrooms for art, music, the humanities, education, and the social sciences? How could I not be in wonder when I attended student assemblies including Sunday vespers services, concerts, recitals, and theatrical productions in the B.N. Duke Auditorium, with its nine hundred seats, a concert grand piano, and Hammond electric organ? Added to these facilities were a gymnasium for women, a men's gymnasium with a swimming pool, a "practice cottage" for senior women in home economics, five residence halls, a new science building, a refectory, a college and law school library, faculty houses, the president's house, tennis courts, and an athletic stadium.

Even in 2009, historians in higher education laud the fact that in the 1940s and 1950s, North Carolina College for Negroes had a coterie of gifted scholars who would be a credit to any college in the land.

Aside from the age factor, my self-portrait as a freshman at North Carolina College for Negroes looked something like this:

My career interest was medical illustration, reflecting my fascination
with the work of medical illustrators at Duke Hospital. I acquired this

interest when I worked part time with Carlin P. Graham, a father surrogate who doubled as a hospital maintenance worker and self-employed professional photographer.

I majored in biology, minored in art, and took the required core-curriculum courses in English, algebra, social science, and physical education. (History was categorized as a social science.) I envisioned a career in which I would combine my interests in biology and art. I had never seen an African American medical illustrator. Nor had I seen one of any ethnic minority. My world was so circumscribed that I came to believe that there would be no place for an African American medical illustrator at any time or in any place. In time, I abandoned this career interest altogether.

I declined fraternity pledge club invitations to membership because I knew too little about them to make an informed decision about which one to join, if I joined one at all.

My stepfather was inducted into the U.S. Army in December 1943. Mama, my brothers, and I were closely knit. We kept our needs and wants in sensible perspective. We owned a black, ten-year-old Buick, which Mama drove.

For transportation to school, I rode buses contracted by the City of Durham with Duke Power Company. I hated the racially segregated rides and got a peculiar sense of relief each time I transferred from a bus marked Lakewood Park and boarded a bus marked Fayetteville Street. The fare, one way, was five cents.

I loved campus life, perhaps too much. I soon came to the realization that I could earn passing grades without sustained, disciplined study, a skill I would not acquire until later, when I was in the U.S. Army.

I enjoyed participating in the college choir, especially at Sunday vespers services. Miss Ruth Gillum was the choral director. During the choir's first rehearsal of the year, Miss Gillum came to the tenor section and gave ear to seatmate Ernest McAdams and me. "Isn't this wonderful?" she exclaimed, evidently pleased to have our new, uninhibited voices. Ernest and I have recalled this experience with considerable delight through the years.

Although Miss Gillum referred to Ernest and me as "wonderful" new-comers to the choir, neither of us was good enough to be given solo parts. That distinction in the tenor section went to Arthur Gibson, an upper-classman from Gary, Indiana. Gibson's voice was smooth and melodious, a voice that made me glad to be in the choir so I could hear him sing, even in rehearsals.

I have been unable to recall selections in which Gibson was the soloist. But I do have a clear recollection of an African American spiritual in which Clarence Newsome, then a junior from Ahoskie, North Carolina, was the soloist. My recollection was unbelievably strong, but I called Newsome in the spring of 2002 for confirmation.

Yes, he was the soloist when the choir sang the spiritual at vespers services. "That was a long time ago, Walt, a very long time," he said. "I am amazed that you remember it." . . . Even though it was Clarence Newsome who sang the solo part, it is unlikely that he has hummed or sung the spiritual to himself over the years as often as I have. The refrain:

> I'm going down to the river of Jordan.
> I'm going down to the river of Jordan some of these days.
> I'm going down to the river of Jordan,
> I'm going down to the river of Jordan some of these days.
> I'm going to run and never get weary . . .
> I'm going to sit at the welcome table . . .
> I'm going to see my loving mother . . .
> I'm going to see my loving father . . .
> I'm going to see my loving Jesus . . .

The college was chartered as a religious institution and remained so until its name change in 1925. However, it was true to its religious heritage during my freshman year, and indeed throughout my undergraduate years. The statement on "Religious Activities" in the college catalog for 1942–1943 is indicative:

> The college, although non-sectarian, feels that no institution, which fails to emphasize religion, is fulfilling its mission to humanity. Education has for its ideal the fitting of the individual for life. Unless one has spiritual discernment and moral appreciation, one is not prepared for social responsibility. Education, therefore, must address itself to the problem of training and directing the emotions as well as the intellect.
>
> To this ideal, this institution is pledged. It endeavors to provide a wholesome religious atmosphere for its students, free from all sectarian bias.

113

Even though I was only sixteen, my classmates and I found pleasure in the custom of instructors addressing us as "Mr." and "Miss." We felt that these salutations helped to fortify us from the insults of white people who refused to address African American adults courteously, especially in the South.

I rejoiced that all students at North Carolina College for Negroes were presumed by their instructors to be initially able to achieve success in their academic pursuits no matter the artificial distinctions of social class or residency, and I was enthralled with the unending opportunities to develop friendships and acquaintances with students from different towns and cities from North Carolina—and, perhaps more exciting from my perspective, from other states and regions.

WALTER M. BROWN is Emeritus Professor of Education and the first dean of the School of Education at North Carolina Central University. His PhD from NCCU is the first awarded by an Historically Black College in America. A World War II veteran, he was a training officer for Volunteers in Service for America, division chief for the U.S. Department of Labor, and a senior consultant with management consulting firms. He is co-author of *The North Carolina Alphabet,* with Durham artist Pamela George. This excerpt is from *I Walked the Sloping Hills: A Memoir.*

Out of the Frying Pan

Duke Hospital—1970

MARGARET RICH

I THOUGHT THE HARD PART was over when I had gotten away from a bad marriage and the Great Dismal Swamp, that lonesome part of Eastern North Carolina, where the four-year-old marriage was made worse. As long as I had my baby girls, ages three and one and a half, I would be fine. We would be fine. It was 1970, and I only knew one person who was divorced, my best friend's mother: a South Carolina version of Zsa Zsa Gabor. I knew I couldn't pull *that* off, but I just had to leave that isolated place and the concrete pumpkin shell my husband tried to keep me in. I didn't care if I only had a high school diploma. I would manage.

There were many reasons, based on the way I was glued together, that I should have liked my new job in a research lab a lot better than the mind-numbing boredom of my first job of two months duration, filing at Duke Hospital. But during my indoctrination when the procedure for the "cardiac puncture" went sideways for Nancy, the hardboiled technologist who was training me, I watched her matter-of-factly tear a chicken's head off, rip its ribcage open, and show me its heart, still beating. I couldn't help but identify with that chicken as I desperately tried to refigure what was reasonable to expect in my new life. In that moment Alma rescued me from a rash decision — I was on ready-to-run-out-of-there.

As if sent by a god, pretty Alma appeared in the doorway of the lab to deliver me from Nancy. Alma was the secretary of Dr. Hurd, the head of the lab. In a charming foreign accent she asked if I had a moment to meet the other people who worked for Dr. Hurd.

Stepping into the hallway with Alma, I felt restored to an equilibrium that could handle another look at what medical research was about. We walked to the lab where the tissue culture end of the operation was in business. I was introduced to Dr. Robineau and his assistants: Jean, Natalie ("Nat"), and Mrs. Dodson. Dr. Robineau didn't match my idea of a scientist. Starched white lab coat aside, he looked more like a street fighter — a dueling scar on his cheek.

"Call me Al," he said.

He was wearing a cloth operating room cap, like Dr. Kildare, cocked someway all his own. He glanced up from the brown-bagged lunch on his desk and smiled.

"I guess you've met Nancy."

Was the word out that a new person was on board? Or did I look traumatized?

"I think we better keep her down here with us." He nodded to Jean and Nat.

Was that possible? I hoped it was, without an inkling of how Dr. Robineau's lab fit into the picture of Dr. Hurd's research.

"Go to lunch and we'll show you the ropes when you get back," he said.

Alma and I became friends-for-life on our first of many walks away from the Bell Building, a shortcut through Duke Hospital, and over to the Dope Shop on campus. We flew through the Davison Building, the old administrative offices of the medical school, and the entrance to the hospital that led out to the campus. We hurried down the worn, stone steps and across the tree-lined quad that spread out like the arms of a cross in front of Duke Chapel.

115

At the student soda fountain, in the basement of the West Union Building, Alma chose a wrapped sandwich. I had lost my appetite months ago. A cigarette was all I ever wanted, but I knew I should eat something. The idea of a chicken salad sandwich was nauseating and so was the pimento cheese—how could I eat anything with red in it, now? I got a bag of potato chips and a ginger ale, something I liked when I was sick. Alma then led me to her rock, a good place to sit, in the near side of Duke Gardens. From Alma's rock we looked out to the fishpond below and up to the wisteria pergola at the top of a long, terraced partier.

In late September it was still hot, but the days were noticeably shorter, relieving everything green from the stress of August. Even a few degrees shy of triple-digit heat were welcome to every living thing. The dogwood leaves were beginning to lose chlorophyll and show a preview of color that signals, if only subliminally, the beginning of the brilliance of autumn in North Carolina. The fragrance of tea olive was everywhere and velvety magnolia pods were getting fat, pink, and bursting with shiny red seeds.

Change was in the air outside and inside the hospital. The fiscal year at the medical school began the first of July, so by September medical students and residents who took up their next positions were getting adjusted to their new lives. Although I wasn't an official part of the medical school I was the same age as these graduate students. Being connected, if only chronologically, felt exciting as I moved along the same corridors with the new class of medical students, interns, and residents hustling to their appointed rounds among their legendary professors.

So many stories were floating around about Dr. Stead, chairman of the Department of Medicine, who was a standout in word and deed—always quoted, always everywhere in the hospital—loved, feared, and respected. *The patient* was his primary consideration. I liked knowing that about him. Seeing patients on rounds, Dr. Stead was famous for asking a young doctor in training, "What do you think this patient needs?" There would be a considered opinion offered by the student about what tests to order or what syndrome certain symptoms may indicate. Then Dr. Stead would weigh in with his learned opinion: "What this patient really needs is a doctor."

He also had one of his oft-quoted lines printed and taped to the ceiling of his office: "Life is hard." When an intern or resident had any extraordinary circumstance to negotiate about the schedule—three days on, one day off; my wife is having a baby; the sky fell down... *anything*—Dr. Stead wouldn't have to say a word. He just pointed to the ceiling. The rest of the quote that everybody knew was: "But folks get mixed up on whether a thing is hard and whether a thing is bad." Being in the midst of a place where so much was expected of people kept me from feeling sorry for myself and whining.

Alma wanted to know all about my children. I told her about the happiest day of my life, when Gibson was born—right behind us on Sims Ward. When they rolled Gibson and me out of the delivery room to see my husband, he and half his fraternity were there—the last people I wanted to see, or to see me, at that moment. Now that the picture of how I thought my life would be was shattered, it made me feel good to keep the happy parts of my memories. Alma made me promise to let her meet Gibson and Mary soon. I tried to imagine them in their routine at nursery school—it would be naptime.

On our way back to the Bell Building, Alma filled me in on the characters in the lab, primarily Nancy who I had guessed was Dr. Hurd's right-hand man. *Don't cross her* was the drift. I got it. And I would do my best to make myself indispensable to the people I had met in the other lab.

Alma showed me the bulletin board in the Davison Building where the interns and residents tacked up want ads for part-time work or odd jobs. I wrote down the phone number of a grad student's wife who wanted to take care of children in her apartment. My daughters would need a sitter on Saturday mornings. Everybody in Dr. Hurd's labs worked six days a week. "Only forty hours," Dr. Hurd had told me, "but stretched over six days instead of five." And he didn't want to be "nickeled-and-dimed about overtime." It rarely happened that anyone left the lab early to make up for the Saturday hours.

I shortly learned that the only people who worked for Dr. Hurd on the *technical end* were unskilled people like me who only had a high school education. Mrs. Dodson had less than that. During the Depression, she quit school in the eighth grade to go to work sewing toes in stockings at a hosiery mill. Her job washing glassware for Dr. Robineau was an improvement over production work at Erwin Mill. I think the man in the personnel office could tell I fit the profile of someone who could hang in there with Dr. Hurd—*desperate* written all over what was *not* in my resume. I couldn't quit, but I made up my mind that it would take more than Nancy and Dr. Hurd to upset my plan to be at Duke with so many possibilities all around me.

While the children seemed to be making a good adjustment to day care, I grieved not being able to watch them every day, every hour.

The tissue culture lab was where I spent my days. Jean and Nat were in charge of most of the activity in the sterile room, and Mrs. Dodson was in charge of washing the mountains of glassware their activities generated. My primary job was at the sink next to Mrs. Dodson, rinsing—ten times with tap water, five times with distilled. In the meantime, I washed everything else: counters, walls, cabinets, windows. I wanted to go the extra mile and be cheerful doing it so they'd keep me.

Jean became my special buddy in the lab. Tall and sturdy, she had dark brown hair cropped in natural curls around her open, generous face. She laughed easily. Nat, on the other hand, was short and less forthcoming than the others. She was shy, I think.

Nat and Dr. Robineau seemed to be a sort of team. Jean took me under her wing and even invited the children and me to her house on the odd Sunday. She brought me hand-me-down clothes from her nieces for Gibson and Mary—soft, broken-in, corduroy overalls that didn't need ironing like the dresses my mother sent.

Jean explained what she and Nat were doing in the sterile room, a small, glassed-in area large enough for a three-by-five metal table and the two of them seated across from each other on swivel stools.

The viruses were grown in a culture of chicken serum and certain nutrients in two-liter Erlenmeyer flasks with a flat bottom, a conical body, and a cylindrical neck (the kind I'd seen in laboratories in horror movies and *The Nutty Professor*). As the viruses multiplied, they had to be divided into clean flasks with fresh serum and nutrients. When the viral count got to a certain number, the flasks would be brought to the sterile atmosphere in our lab to be divided. Nat and Jean would pour half of the old culture into the new medium in two new flasks. In the process the tops of the flasks had to be drawn across an open flame—a Bunsen burner on the table between them—to prevent introducing any contaminant into the culture. The discarded flasks that had held the older medium generated all the glassware Mrs. Dodson and I had to wash. More and more were always on the way.

In addition to my rinsing duties I was taught how to make the stoppers that were placed inside the clean, empty flasks before they were put in the autoclave, a large sterilizing oven that looked like a bank vault in the side of the wall. While Mrs. Dodson boiled up her side of the industrial metal sink—it had a heating element under it—I made the stoppers. Nothing was wasted. I cut the brown paper that wrapped our laundered lab dresses and lab coats into approximately eight-inch squares. I cut squares of gauze about the same size and stuffed them with wads of cotton to place in the mouth of the flasks. The brown paper was then placed over these stoppers and tied around the top of the flask with string. I wrapped the string twice around the neck of the flask then tied a bow, one length of the string decidedly longer, so that Jean and Nat could untie it easily in the duet they did at the table in the sterile room.

Mrs. Dodson, on the front end of our assembly line, was the slowest woman in the world. She was sweet-natured and sweet-looking with blue hair and a permanent. She had had it with production work after all those years at the hosiery mill, where workers were paid by the number of garments they turned out. She was not inclined to hurry anymore. I couldn't do anything until she got the ball rolling. I had to wait while she put the detergent in the sink, wait for the water to boil, wait for her to add cold water when the glassware had boiled long enough, and wait while she put on her rubber gloves so she could put her hands in the water. My feet were tap dancing while I waited for Mrs. Dodson—the top half of me leaning on the sink with my elbows.

And she hummed. She hummed the same two notes all day long. I tried to get her to talk but she had created a refuge of silence for herself that was impervious to my inroads of conversation. I didn't mind being quiet, but the humming was insufferable and unstoppable. I deviously thought of suggesting some muzak like "The Little Nash Rambler," whose *beep, beeps* keep getting faster and faster.

One day I said, "What are you humming over there, Mrs. Dodson?" I saw Jean, Nat, and Dr. Robineau do an about-face and bend double to stifle their laughter. Maybe they had been placing bets about how long I could stand it.

"Oh, I don't know," Mrs. Dodson said. "I'm just humming."

"Well, maybe we could think of something to sing that we both know," I said. "Do you know any hymns?" She just smiled and shook her head. "How about 'Oh My Darling Clementine'?"

I got nowhere trying to distract Mrs. Dodson from the humming, but Mrs. Leathers did need some help in her headquarters up the hall. I let Mrs. Dodson get a running start on washing bottles while Mrs. Leathers showed me how to wash slides.

Mrs. Leathers was short and spritely with white hair, neatly quaffed and held in place with an invisible hairnet. She walked like a dwarf—a kind of side-to-side action—and was built like a milk carton with arms and legs. We sat in her room, which was like a big kitchen with a large table in the middle, padded and covered with a clean sheet. Cleaning slides was a tedious job and took a long time to place the used glass slides in metal racks, notched with thin slits. When the racks were filled we dipped the trays into tall vats of dichromic acid. The fumes from the acid could put runs in your stockings and a tiny splash could put a sizable hole in your clothes. Mrs. Leathers was very careful. I *learned* to be careful, after enough times of ruining my pantyhose—the most expensive part of my wardrobe. When I had ruined a few pairs with a run in only one leg, I got the idea to cut off the legs with the runs in them and wear two pairs with one good leg in each. Wearing two pairs felt tight and made it hard to sit for long, but it saved money.

While we lined up the slides in the racks she told me about her grown, mentally retarded son whom she cared for by herself since her husband had died. She had to get to work an hour early, due to the intricacies of getting her son to his caretakers and the limitations of the bus sched-ule. She was matter-of-fact in the face of such hardship, a cheerful person, pleasant to be with. She moved fast, distributing glassware of all kinds to every lab in the building and only sat down to lay slides in their racks. She had a chalkboard on the wall to keep track of whose glassware was in the autoclave and which labs needed to be *collected.*

It came to me out of the blue, while I was sitting with Mrs. Leathers, that I didn't know where all the chicken serum came from. Could it be frozen somewhere? I hadn't noticed any chickens being brought up to Nancy's lab. I hadn't seen Nancy at all unless she had a reason to come to our lab to speak with Dr. Robineau. I lived in dread that my job would be put on the line by Nancy asking me to help her again.

As the days grew shorter and the autumn leaves had blown off the trees, there was a buzz of excitement in the lab about the state fair *and* about the annual trip to the chicken slaughterhouse to collect chicken blood. A couple of medical students and researchers from other labs were going, and so were Nat, Jean, and Dr. Robineau. I wanted to go.

"No, you don't want to go," they all said.

"Yes, I do. I really want to go."

I wanted to get away from Mrs. Dodson's humming. I wanted a change of pace. I wanted to be a part of the laughter they all laughed when the planning got down to brass tacks: big rubber trashcans, aluminum grates, sheets of gauze. I pictured us all playing cards and having a big time while the chickens did the usual bleeding they did before they got to the grocery store neatly packaged.

I should have had reservations when they ordered me a Sears Roebuck plastic rain suit — with a hood. But I definitely wanted to go.

I had to make special arrangements for the children, so I could meet everybody at the crack of dawn in the Bell Building parking lot. On the appointed day I gathered up Gibson and Mary in their pajamas and coats with a little suitcase and took them to the woman who looked after them on Saturday mornings. I kissed them goodbye and felt guilty for disturbing their dreams.

The lab crew traveled over to the chicken slaughterhouse in a caravan. When we arrived at our location Dr. Robineau got busy assimilating all the paraphernalia on a loading dock. The regular employees of the slaughter-house were just getting to work and turning lights on inside. I hung with the women who were suiting up. I put on my plastic rain gear. I thought the rain suit might be overkill. I still didn't think I'd be anywhere near a chicken. Who brought the cards?

I looked into the room where the rubber trashcans were going. It had white ceramic tile up to the ceiling. Dr. Robineau handed the trashcans over a two-foot high tiled threshold (like a footbath at a public swimming pool) to the medical students inside. They strung up two clotheslines on both sides of the room and hung a thousand sheets of gauze over them. Aluminum grates went on top of the trashcans. Two or three layers of gauze sheeting went on top of the grates.

The chickens were backed up to the far loading dock in wooden crates like you see traveling down the highway — feathers flying. I could see how it worked: The chickens were uncrated; their feet were clamped close together; then they were hung feet first from a metal conveyer belt. The chickens traveled upside down to a bicycle tire that rolled over their heads and forced their necks into a rotary blade that slit their throats; the not-entirely-beheaded chickens then traveled the length of the tiled room at a pace that allowed them to bleed out before they moved through an open window to the inside of the building where they were plucked, cut up, and packaged. To collect the serum it was necessary for people to be in the tiled room to change the gauze filters so that chicken blood could collect in the trashcans. It didn't take long for the gauze coverings to become matted with feathers and excrement. As the upside-down chickens moved through the room (and because they could not walk around, like they are supposed to), they just shook harder and harder. It was awful.

I didn't expect to be asked to go in there, even though I had volunteered to come along. I thought they wanted to see if I was a good sport—up to a point. But they gave me what they gave everybody else: several paper operating-room caps to wear over my hair and under my plastic hood and a thick paper mask to wear over my mouth and nose. Dr. Robineau handed me a pair of his black galoshes, several sizes too big. I held out for this to be the last part of the test of my good sport-ness, believing at the last minute I would be pardoned, and excused. The research staff went in. The medical students went in. I went in.

As I stepped over the tiled threshold, warm chicken blood slung across my face, I slipped—took an extra half step in the big boots—and tears streamed down my face. It was a good thing, too, because those tears kept the chicken shit out of my eyes. Nobody could see I was crying because of the mask. I didn't want them to see me. My tears dried up as the initial affront abated and I found a more advantageous place to stand. I went to work changing the gauze. All day I stayed in there waiting—looking toward the doorway—to be invited out. Everybody else took a break—went out and came back—I stayed in through lunch (they had brought food, but I couldn't think about eating). At the end of the day, the chickens stopped coming; the rubber trashcans of blood were loaded into Dr. Robineau's truck; and we began to hose off and peel off our gear. The mask over my mouth and nose was like a used Kotex pad; wisps of my hair stuck to my face with dried blood. Jean gave me a hug after she cleaned me up around the edges with the washcloths she had known to bring. I was speechless. And stayed speechless when the group adjourned to the Top Hat, a pizza place on Ninth Street, for a beer.

Hell, seconds ago, I looked like a pizza.

I went for a beer and a chance to decompress before I re-entered my life. That's where the laughter of the group started. Not mine.

The following March, I was fired on my twenty-fourth birthday. I didn't ask why. I thought I knew why. My good sport attitude went to hell after that day of collecting serum at the chicken slaughterhouse. Amid the backdrop of life and death at Duke Hospital and the chicken slaughterhouse, something in me was born. I couldn't be irresponsible enough to quit my job, but now that I was fired, I felt like celebrating. My resume was a little less thin and from that day forward, no matter how mixed up I got about whether a thing was hard or whether a thing was bad, I could always say: "At least this is not as bad as bleeding chickens."

Born in South Carolina, **MARGARET RICH** spent most of her adult life in North Carolina, with some long detours to California and England, and most recently to Vermont where she earned an MFA in creative writing at Bennington College. This story is excerpted from her memoir-in-progress.

Views in Fiction

Last Days, Old Ballpark

CLYDE EDGERTON

PRETEND THAT THE FINGERNAIL on the fourth finger of your right hand is the face of a clock. Find the 10 o'clock position. Just beyond the fingernail and on to the skin of my father's finger was a growth that looked like a tiny baby finger. When I was a little boy, he'd hold it down to me and I'd study it, touch it, look up at him.

"Does it hurt?" I'd say.

"No."

I asked him about it many times, and he always explained that he got it from bowling, from spinning duck balls off that fourth finger. He had a small trophy, a trophy of a bowling pin. The inscription was "Durham Champion—1932."

Daddy grew up outside Durham, where he was born in 1902 on a tobacco farm. He started smoking cigarettes when he was twelve years old—that would be in 1914, before World War I. Late in life he stopped smoking, but in 1980 emphysema finally whipped him down for good. The day before he died, I washed his back with warm, soapy water as he sat on the side of his hospital bed, and his seventy-seven-year-old shoulder blades seemed to be just under the skin, without muscles.

Tobacco had an early, and last, say.

He was about five-feet-six and a little overweight. He never talked much about himself, and in a group he was almost always quiet, always sitting in the back of any crowd, in the very back at church—in a cane-bottom chair he'd pulled in from somewhere. But he did like to tell this baseball story: In 1924, when he was playing second base for Roy May's Service Station, a semi-pro team in Durham, a man offered him a chance to play minor league baseball in Henderson, North Carolina. The pay would be $50 a week—big money. At that time, he was still living and working on the family tobacco farm.

He went to his parents and asked them (he was twenty-two years old) if he could go to Henderson and play ball.

His mother said no, he was needed on the farm.

So he stayed home.

Early 1950s. An hour or so before a Bulls' game in town we would be off in our green two-door '49 Ford. I would sit in the front seat with Daddy and watch him change gears. He was not an aggressive driver—he wound it up in first gear, then dropped it into third.

Uncle Clem, my mother's brother who lost his left arm in World War I and lived with us, would go along, dressed up, bathed, and shaved. He could tie his shoes with one hand and he'd put a matchbox under his stub and strike a match when he smoked his cigar. He played baseball for the Durham Hosiery Mill right after he returned from the war—caught the ball in his gloved right hand, flipped the ball up, dropped the glove, caught the ball, and threw.

We might pick up Uncle Clyde, who'd also be dressed up—in slacks and a shirt pressed by his sister, my Aunt Ivaleen. He'd smell like after-shave and Listerine. Uncle Clyde was my father's brother and lived with Aunt Ivaleen and her husband, Uncle Corbitt. Occasionally Uncle Corbitt would go along. He's the one who'd give me a stick of chewing gum. Uncle Clyde and Uncle Clem were the least-church-going members in our family. Thus the ball game—with them along—had a faint, but ever-present and wonderfully pleasurable aura of sin.

We drove into town. I was all eyes, and to me, any building taller than two stories was mammoth. We'd pass the tobacco factories and smell the honey-sweet smell of tobacco that hung in the streets near the tobacco factories—a heavy, musky, succulent smell I've always loved—nothing like the smell of burning tobacco.

The Durham Bulls were named after "Bull Durham" tobacco. Without tobacco, the city of Durham may have been only a crossroads—no base-ball team, no Durham Athletic Park. My father may have lived longer.

Daddy would buy our tickets at the gate, then I'd hold his hand—my eyes at his belt—and we'd walk into the stadium, find seats on the third-base side, in the stands, about a third of the way up. I'd ask him if I could go to the top of the stands and look out back across the street at the "fire building." He'd say, Yes.

The fire building behind the park was (and still is) a building the size— at ground level—of one large room, but it's five stories high. It was one of the most dramatic buildings imaginable for me when I was five or six because I'd been told that firemen practiced jumping out of its windows. Back then, several firemen would stand in a circle on the ground at the base of burning building—holding something like a large trampoline. A trapped fireman or a resident would jump from a window onto this device. My mind carries images of firemen jumping from the fire build-ing, though I'm almost sure I never saw this happen. I even somehow almost remember that building on fire. I believed back then that because the building was brick it could somehow be set afire with no harm to the structure. That building helped establish my early ambition to be a fireman—a fireman by day, a baseball player by night.

Uncle Clem and Uncle Clyde would be smoking cigars by the time I got back to my seat and we'd all sit and watch the game. Uncle Clyde would give me the little paper ring that fit around his cigar and I'd slip it onto my finger.

I remember looking out to the brightly lit field, having no idea what the game was about. I can even remember not being sure which way the players ran after they hit the ball—to first base or to third. I remember asking if a batter was out when a fielder caught a hit ball on first bounce.

The Town Speaks

I am old red brick, and tobacco warehouses, and the new glass buildings, and drugs, murder, banks, asphalt, cars, trucks, trains, daycare, Baptists, Methodists, Catholics, Jews, Hindus, atheists, lawyers, segregation, integration, buses, social work, negotiation, computers, cyberspace, and in 1994 a tall new $43-million-and-counting modern prison down by the tracks where men used to hang out and burn wood in barrels, drink wine, and tell funny stories, sad stories of deception, before late at night, curling up in ones and twos and sleeping; and I am also the hope of a merging school system born of tears and rage through stiff resistance always and forever embracing the irrational and the dead solid-clear hatred of the different, but especially fearing the fresh opportunity for dangerous rebirth; music, new restaurants, the blues now but also mainly always when the blues was the blues in Hayti with Sonny Terry and Brownie McGhee ("My Baby Done Changed the Lock on the Door," "East Coast Blues") and the Reverend Gary Davis, who was the patient teacher of more blues musicians than you can shake a stick at.

And now, *whoa,* now Durham is the City of Medicine. The Blues is medicine, but medicine ain't the blues. Hospitals, doctors all over.

A home to Duke University. Or is it?

The train is Amtrak, and no more logs and planks lie helter-skelter along the streets. Little trees are planted in concrete, near the Carolina Theatre — restored; and downtown is not nearly vacant, like they say, but the ones still there don't count to the pink and brown people in blue and gray suits and black lace-up shoes, holding clicking ballpoint pens. The caring capitalists are out of downtown. The action of this world is now in the mall in the mall in the mall, an environment of clarity — clean, clear, controlled, and safe, with no surprises. No surprises. A place for adventurous senior citizens to walk for health.

Beyond the Lucky Strike smokestack, the water tower, the old buildings, lie the malls. But still here in the middle of all the old brick is Durham Athletic Park, still here in 1994 after fifty-five years.

The Stadium Speaks

I am Durham Athletic Park, established 1939.

Many *leagues* have been hosted by me and earlier Durham ballparks. They include: North Carolina League, North Carolina State League, North Carolina Association, Tar Heel League, Coastal Plain League, Piedmont League, Bi-State League, and others. Older ballparks are forgotten and cannot be resurrected except in the hearts of those who remember. So it will be with me and those that follow. We will have our moments of drama in a *real* time and place, not drama *constructed* on stage or screen or in a book, and we will host people who are happy and sad, those relieved by, and those worried by, the art and science of what was once America's pastime.

The Fan

Also when I was a little, I marveled at the sets of ballpark night lights way up at the top of the light poles. These days there are only ten or twelve giant lights per pole. Back then there were thirty or forty small ones. Sometimes, especially if it started raining, one would burst and down would fall, almost in slow motion, a cascade of sparkling glass. Ball players sitting or standing under the loud *pop* would scatter, eyes held purposefully to the ground. These breaking lights, leaving a smoking black hole in the brightness, were among the most dramatic sights of my childhood.

One of the first matters I got straight was that the good players, the Bulls, were dressed in white and the foreigners were dressed in gray. I found out we were pulling for only one team—the Bulls—not the other team. They were strangers. They looked lonely.

When I was a boy, the Negro Leagues were in their latter days. I never saw them play. My loss was understood by many—unfortunately, sadly—as necessary. Writers, photographers, filmmakers, and the players are helping us all learn about the drama, the heartache, the love of the game on their fields during those times of earlier racism.

The Stadium

Three big baseball parks in Durham, North Carolina, before me:

George Lynn Ballpark
Doherty Park
El Toro

. . . for organized baseball, meaning you pay to get inside to see a team play that is the one official team for the city of Durham. Not all those ragtag teams.

George Lynn Ballpark, laid out beside a cemetery—other side of town. There, the first game of organized baseball in Durham was played in 1902. In that very first game, Pinckney Boles broke his ankle sliding into second base in the bottom of the third inning. He waited too late to slide and the middle rear cleat on his left shoe caught the outside corner of the bag. He walked off the field under his own power, sat in the dugout until the swelling made them send for Doctor Clements.

Doherty Park, built in 1910, owned by electric company, occupied by Durham Bulls—1913. A gambling ring worked every Saturday afternoon, run by the Hargrove boys out of Leesville Road community—three brothers. A little man from Greensboro (only five-feet-two and 107 pounds), Mr. Gerald Simpson, who found himself called to police work by the Lord, infiltrated the ring to stop the sinning, but he was won over and held close by the charm of the Hargrove boys and the fun and daring and drama of it all, and ended up getting shot in both knees behind the visiting team's dugout.

Women stopped coming to the ball games at Doherty Park because of hearing the g.d. and other words, gambling, trash, mud, messy restrooms, loud nasty men and boys.

Now my predecessor—El Toro—brand new all-wood stadium, built in 1926 by Bulls owner and investors, built in a new place, here where I now rest, on eight acres, to clean up the sport. At dedication, July 1926, Judge Kenasaw Mountain Landis, United States baseball commissioner, famous man, rode the live bull mascot on the playing field. Newsreels of it played in movie houses all across the good old USA.

Next: hard times. Depression. Ballpark owners in debt sold the ballpark to an investment company. In 1933 Mr. and Mrs. John Sprunt Hill gave

Durham $20,000 to buy a park—and the city did—but no ball games for 1934 and 1935: Depression.

Games resumed in 1936 and "El Toro" changed to "Durham Athletic Park"—what Mr. Hill wanted.

But fire would wake up the groundskeeper, Walter Clarence Williams, asleep on his cot under the stands on the warm night of June 17, 1939, at 11:15, and run him through the center-field gate and into the street. The stadium burned down while folks in pajamas watched for two hours with firelight reflected in their faces. Industrious onlookers sold ham sandwiches, pickles, milk, and beer.

The fire department didn't have a chance. All that dry wood. It was a big bright fire.

Out of ashes, looking just about exactly like my predecessor, except not wood anymore, I am built of concrete and steel. I was built to last a hundred years. My first baseball game, April 7, 1940. Cincinnati beat Boston in a Sunday afternoon exhibition game. 5,574 fans. It was a big day.

Now 1995—I'm a nostalgic old ballpark. This year—the last year. The last last year. Then I'll be no more for minor league baseball.

A new stadium rises up—over by the expressway. My successor.

Will I become as forgotten as El Toro? As Doherty, as George Lynn? Where were they built anyway?

Tobacco factories stand around here, old friends and enemies, and other buildings and warehouses, mostly old friends. The auto shops, old buildings, Vega Metals, Green's Grill, Liberty Warehouse, now closed to tobacco, now holding old wooden chairs and chicken wire and manikins. Storage.

In season the tobacco smells sweet, heavy, honey-sweet in the day and night below, above, and around other fumes and smoke smells. The Lucky Strike smokestack, red brick, there forever, stands against the sky, the western sky, home to Marlboro man, the sky that is light longest—in the late day colors of red, then purple, then orange, pink, yellow, maroon, and gray, then gradually to dark, a warm baseball night with Big Sky above, my lights light the baseball field—white chalk-dusted bases, first, second, third, tan-orange infield dirt, green infield grass, chalk white foul lines, green outfield grass—all light up, lighter and lighter as gray streets and gray buildings dim in spite of street lights surrounded by tree leaves moving in warm breezes; all the land outside dims and dims and dims, until the world is dark and the ball diamond is one bright, sacred light on this ancient dark Earth, beamed at the speed of light into the full dark void, so that I ride the crest of a light wave, forever, in spite of all the confusion left behind.

The bases come up for the last time. The groundskeeper pulls the handle and the lights go out. The bugs, thousands of bugs, hold to the heat of the darkened lights, then head toward shaded street lights nearby, arrive, circle and loop, flip, flop, and fly, until the eastern sky lightens, and birds begin to move, sing, and chatter, looking for breakfast.

Hot, sunny, summer *dayz* die off slowly, fading into a warm *bazeball* night with Big Sky big above, gray *streetz* and gray *buildingz* all around dimming in spite of street *lightz,* some surrounded by tree *leavez* moving shade *spotz* on *sidewalkz* in warm evening *breezez,* and all the land of North Carolina slowly *dimz,* until all the world is dark. I dream back to when the *Bullz* took the field here, the ball *diamxndz* light in *thiz* ancient dark *wxrld, shxxtzzz* a bright sacred beam *zzz zzzz* the dark *vxid, zzzzzzzzz fxrever* at the speed of light. Leaving all the confusion behind.

Born in Durham, **CLYDE EDGERTON** is the author of ten novels, including *Walking Across Egypt, Lunch at the Piccadilly,* and *The Night Train.* He has been a Guggenheim Fellow and five of his novels have been *New York Times* Notable Books. A member of the Fellowship of Southern Writers, he teaches creative writing at the University of North Carolina Wilmington. This story is adapted from an unpublished book by Clyde Edgerton and Jean-Christian Rostagni, commemorating the Durham Athletic Park.

Home Is a Cup of Coffee

CARL W. KENNEY II

"HAS ANYONE SEEN STICK?"

The silence in the room said more than words could. The silence of sadness, the silence of concern for the man we all knew who stood outside every day, waiting for pocket change as customers entered the Bean Traders on Ninth Street. Stick was different from the other homeless people in the neighborhood who would aggressively approach people with a heartbreaking story meant to encourage giving.

"No, I haven't seen him," Shana, one of the baristas, responded.

"I was thinking the same thing this morning," Nathan, the head of the dojo, said as he pulled papers from a briefcase.

The room was filled with worry for the homeless man known best for his name and demeanor. It was one of those bitter cold days where people feared frostbite, a scary time for those who lived among the trees and listened to the sounds of nature before going to sleep.

"You know the church took down the tents," Tony added.

"That's a shame. Where they supposed to stay in the cold?" My mind swelled with thoughts of protecting those too weak to fight.

"They say the city forced them to take them down because of a code violation," Tony continued.

Tony sat as though glued to his seat. His eyes fixed on a place beyond view. His tears flowed from somewhere inside him, between pain and fear. His mind seemed trapped in a place he dreaded visiting but couldn't escape, that place where the Boogey Man and the Grim Reaper destroy all hope and toy with the imagination.

The conversation changed when a customer opened the door, bringing with her the cold wind.

"I can't remember it ever being this cold in Durham," she said, grabbing a cup to take the freeze away.

"Yeah, this is why I left Missouri," I said. "Got tired of the snow and cold."

Talk of the cold made it worse. The thought of being able to drive to my warm home left me pondering the comforts of privilege. A few minutes in the cold are enough to challenge the decision to stay out to play. Having a place with heat, a car filled with gasoline, and more than enough to eat are things easily taken for granted.

I couldn't stop thinking about Stick. Most of the people who frequented the Bean Traders knew him. A black man in his early fifties, Stick was part legend and part man to be pitied. His hair and beard were covered with gray, giving him the appearance of one much older. His fashion reflected all things given, yet chosen with care. The bold colors often clashed. Purples and greens and blues wrapped his body like a Soul Train dancer. His style begged attention.

His walk said even more, trapped in an age when cool was bold colors and footsteps danced like James Brown getting down to one of those funky beats.

Stick talked slow, as though his words were set in motion to spit rhymes. His head nodded when people passed on their way to a mocha release. Stick was old-school cool, aching to play with new-school dreams.

Every homeless person has a story. Stick's was filled with the tragedy of consequences. Those old-school ways caught up with him in a way that took his mind on a journey, a one-way ticket. He hadn't been able to find his way back home since. The game of memories had become a war for sanity, a war he lost long ago.

It started when those bold colors defined Stick's vocation. He made money from the lure of women and the obsessions of those too weak to say no. He drove a white Cadillac with red leather interior and a fur covering the steering wheel. Dice dangling from the rearview mirror signaled that this was the man who drove like cool in the summertime — the roll of the dice, each day a gamble.

Stick was a pimp and drug dealer during a time when black men saw those as the best ways to make a living. College wasn't an option and his draft number was low. The fear of going to Vietnam was intensified by the many cousins, uncles, brothers, and friends who came back in black bags.

It was the era after the dream of Martin Luther King Jr. turned into a nightmare. The streets buzzed with black folks complaining about injustice. Afros, handshakes, and songs about change became a way to evoke black pride and power.

It was the year Shirley Chisholm announced her bid for president, the same year the first black man was inducted into the Basketball Hall of Fame. It was the year the movie *The Godfather* was released, and George Wallace was shot, and the first hand-held calculator was introduced. It was the year of Watergate and protests across the nation. It was 1972.

Stick got his one-way ticket out of his home. He lived on McDougald Terrace, within walking distance of North Carolina Central University. The school, established in 1910 by James E. Shepard to educate black ministers and teachers, had just become part of the University of North Carolina system. By the early Seventies, the school was known for teaching the young entrepreneurs who would create Black Wall Street on Parrish Street. NCCU provided the link between Durham's black elite and the dream of education. But it stood, and still stands, in the neighborhood where poverty was the unbroken chain that bound many of its citizens.

Young people with promise took classes on campus, while those across the street waited for government cheese and prayed for the safety of their children. Optimism followed those on one side; getting high lifted the spirits of those on the other. Every now and then, a person from one side would make his or her way to the other, proving the power of bonds beyond normal definition.

One day Stick arrived home on McDougald and pulled a bag of groceries from the trunk of his shiny Cadillac. He held the hand of his three-year-old son as they prepared to take the food inside. It was one of those hot days that made being cool challenging. Stick placed his purple suit jacket in the backseat. The shirt under his vest was soaked with perspiration and his feet ached from the tight grip of his red alligator platform shoes.

"Come on Junior," he commanded, as his boy clutched his hand to cross the street.

"Okay, Daddy."

The day had been filled with fun that reminded Stick that he had a life beyond the work he did to pay the bills. His years at Hillside High School had given him a clear message of what could not be his. His grades, coupled with frequent suspensions, convinced him that life at the college across the street was outside the realm of possibilities.

But Stick knew women and the streets. He rolled the dice every day.

Three kids and two women with needs kept Stick hustling for a living. Deep down he desired more than a fast-paced life where avoiding the police and comforting the politics of the hood were constant tensions. His son kept him focused on why he had to continue. Stick wanted more for his son, more than his own father and mother had given him. More than he gave himself.

Drops of salt water dripped from his brow like ice cream melting in the heat. He paused long enough to check the traffic. A blue Mustang was headed in their direction. The roar of the engine could be heard blocks away. It looked like the driver was racing by himself.

"Hold my hand tight, Junior. They driving crazy," Stick yelled just before the first pop.

Pop, pop, pop, pop. Four shots came from the convertible. Four shots meant to take Stick to that place where fried chicken dinners and potato salad follow the last words spoken about a person's life. He grabbed Junior to shield him from the bullets.

"Damn," he screamed as he opened the door to place his baby boy inside. He carried him close fearing another shot would come. The Mustang made a right turn on the dividing road headed north. He clung to his baby boy until he couldn't hear the roar of the racing car.

"You okay baby! You okay!" No answer. He was afraid to look. His eyes were clutched tight like the grip of his fist. "You okay!" No answer.

"Jesus!" he cried as he opened his eyes. Blood. Blood on his vest. Blood matching the color of his fancy interior. Blood on his hands and face and neck. Blood on his baby boy flowing from his chest. No breath. No movement. Arms limp like meat on the table.

"No, no, not my baby!" He screamed loud as a crowd, packed like sardines, surrounded him.

Stick pulled out the pistol he kept hidden under his seat and began shooting in the air, like his enemy was in the sky. He pulled the trigger until there were no bullets left. He kept pulling, waiting for more to show up. One empty shot after another.

Stick tore the bloodied purple vest and threw it on the ground. A man gone wild, he tore the silk shirt off and covered his bleeding son with it like, as though he were wrapping something precious that needed to be honored. The streets were filled with crying people. Their tears poured with the compassion of those who had seen too many die too soon.

That's when Stick got his one-way ticket. He left that day and never went back home. He lived in the misery of his own guilt, guilt that kept him imprisoned in thoughts of what could have been if not for his life of pimping women and dealing drugs. Revenge kept him locked behind bars of pain. The revenge he felt was not directed at the man in the racecar as much as it was leveled at himself.

That's how the streets became Stick's new home. He said little. He bothered no one. He lived on spare change. A nickel and a quarter at a time, he grabbed enough for the next bottle. Enough to take the pain away. Another bottle of rum or vodka or whatever his coins could purchase. Enough to erase the chill of those memories long enough for him to take another step. It was a long walk to the end of his pain.

"Stick, where are you?"

The temperature outside the Bean Traders had dipped below twenty degrees. The swirl of the wind sounded like a shriek for shelter. What would the night bring? The clock was ticking.

"Stick, where are you?"

I felt a compulsion to pray. The Bean Trader family could commune in faith that Stick would show up before the sunset. Where would we take him? Where had he been? What could we do beyond the quarters we gave to feed his pain? Why did we care?

The door opened bringing in the cold again. There he stood, trembling before us. His eyes revealed massive consumption. No words. Something was wrong. He was hurting deep. Deeper than any of us could understand. His body was frail from absence of will.

Stick.

Everyone was shocked when he started to make his way inside. He never came in. He always stopped others on their way in and asked them to buy him coffee, giving them change to pay. He would stand outside, absorbing the love from the sacred space where people gathered for more than coffee. He stood there every day, silently. He nodded from time to time as those walking down the street handed him change. It was their offering of love to a member of the body of survivors. He stood outside, but he never crossed the boundary between despair and hope.

He respected the space inside, claimed by those with jobs and homes and cars and hope. He refrained from entering the room where those with credibility gather to drink black brew and type on laptop computers. The door was a barrier separating hope from despair — like that road separating a college from public housing.

But today, he had braved his way beyond the barrier, in hope of finding enough compassion to move him past his pain.

He stood frozen by cold and memories. One foot planted inside the door, the other still planted on the sidewalk, on the other side of hope. One foot in, one foot out. This was new pain propelling him to move. This was old pain begging him to stay.

"Stick," Tony screamed.

"Where you been?" Nathan echoed

Everyone jumped to grab their friend. He fell in Tony's arms, knowing he would catch him. Everyone reached for a part of him. It looked like the laying on of hands in the consecration of a bishop. The hands of a community reached out to grab hold of one of their own.

"Sit down, Stick," Laura yelled. The family led him to the green couch. Shana brought a cup of coffee. Room was made for Stick to breathe.

It's strange how home can be found among those so different. Where else could a homeless man find refuge among those with multiple degrees listed on their vita? A college professor, an attorney, doctoral students, the owner of a dojo, and a minister offered comfort on a green couch normally occupied by those with laptops and mochas.

Stick's eyes said all we needed to know. We had stayed longer than usual, waiting for him to come back home. He was there, but home was far away.

Coffeehouses have a way of creating intimate space. The safe limits of common linkage are strengthened by the power of brew coupled with conversation.

"Where are you from? How did you get here?" are the questions that begin the journey to a life of meaning beyond the neat lives we create to protect ourselves from *those people.* It's more than the coffee. It's more than the green couch and aroma of that addictive black brew that take hold of lives once limited by narrow-minded ways.

"You okay, Stick?" everyone wanted to know. Few knew the story behind the man. It didn't matter. Would it change their view of him if they knew the rest?

We waited for Stick to speak. Nothing. No words. No movement beyond a few twitches of his eyelids. His hands clutched the cup of coffee meant to bring warmth to his chilled body. No one moved. A few tears were shed to convey the joy and pain of the moment. Joy that he was there. Pain that no one knew what to do next.

What is worse, the cold or the memories?

Then it happened. He moved. He took a sip of coffee. The cup stayed close enough for the next sip. Then another. Then another, until the cup was empty.

"Where you going, Stick?" Tony asked, begging him not to move.

No answer. No hesitation. He rose from the green couch. One inch at a time. Slow, like he feared what would find him on the other side of the door—the cold.

"You don't have to leave!" Greg blasted, in hope that his words would form a wall of resistance. It didn't work. Stick stepped out, to the other side of warmth. Back to the cold and snow. Back to the darkening night, the sadness of isolation.

We tried to stop him. He left the safety of home to enter the only home he knew—the streets. Those of us still inside, watching, felt a part of home walk away. It was hard to endure the ache of departing for our own homes, places safe from the freeze. How could we, knowing Stick had no home. We couldn't stop him. No one knew what stopping him meant. Where would we take him?

Some tried to hide their tears. Others set them free as they prepared to leave the coffeehouse. We marched like an army in defeat. The sounds of car doors closing boomed like a bass drum at the end of a tragic opera. The churning of engines began and we headed toward those places of comfort far removed from Stick.

Home is a cup of coffee, shared.

CARL W. KENNEY II is a writer and the pastor of Compassion Ministries of Durham, an American Baptist Church he founded over a decade ago. He holds a Master of Divinity from Duke University. His commentary has appeared in the *Herald-Sun, News & Observer, Independent Weekly,* and other publications. He also has published two novels, *Backslide* and *Preacha' Man.* He blogs at rev-elution.blogspot.com.

Wonderland

LEWIS SHINER

(Excerpted from his novel *Black & White*)

 IT WAS THE SPRING of 1964. The office had hit its Friday afternoon stride, windows open to the late March air, cool flowering smells of the North Carolina outdoors replacing stale cigarette smoke. Conversation had fallen off and the room was quiet except for the hum of the fans, the zip of parallel bars, the slap of plastic triangles, the pop of the suction cup on the base of a lead pointer. Maurice, the company's one Negro draftsman, started to hum. The sound, blending with the others, slipped beneath Robert's conscious threshold.

Maurice broke off in mid-note and looked at him. "What are you doing?"

"What?" Robert asked.

"Hey, boss," Maurice yelled in the general direction of Antree's office, where he'd been holed up since lunch. "Come out here!"

"Look, I didn't mean anything," Robert said. It was the opening riff from Coltrane's "Giant Steps" that Maurice had been humming, and Robert realized he'd been whistling along.

Antree emerged into the drafting room, collar open, pink shirtsleeves rolled to the elbow. "What's up?"

"Your boy here listens to Coltrane," Maurice said.

Antree squinted at Robert. "Is that true?"

"Yes," Robert said, pleased and embarrassed.

"Just Coltrane?" Antree asked. "Or anybody else?"

"Miles," Robert said. "Jamal. Dizzy, Bird."

"'Bird,'" Maurice said, shaking his head. "'Bird,' the man calls him. Who said you could call him 'Bird'?"

"Cool it, Maurice," Antree said. Robert was still not used to the way Antree affected Negro slang and clothing. "Everybody calls him Bird. Robert, step into my office." Maurice followed without invitation.

Antree's office was cool and dark, with only a floor lamp in one corner for illumination. Thick drapes hid the window, and wall-to-wall carpet muffled their footsteps. There were framed prints by an artist Robert didn't recognize, full of distorted figures and odd blue colors.

"So tell me, Bobby," Antree said. "How long has this been going on?"

Robert shrugged. "My father was into the swing bands, the early cool stuff. I started listening to bop when I was in Germany. American bands were always touring Europe. Art Taylor and Donald Byrd, Bud Powell with Kenny Clark—they were living over there. I saw Miles in Paris in December of '57 at this tiny little club in St. Germain . . ."

Antree and Maurice looked at each other. "Definitely," Antree said.

"You ever hear Charlie Shavers?" Maurice asked.

"I've got one of his records," Robert said. "*Like Charlie*?"

"Well, tonight," Antree said, "you're going to be seeing him in person."

"He's at the Wonderland Theater," Maurice said.

"But . . . isn't that in Hayti?"

Antree smiled at him as if he were a child. "That's right, Bobby. Hayti."

Robert's emotions felt like crickets, jumping in the cupped hands of his chest. "I can't," he said. "Ruth doesn't even like music, and—"

Antree slid the pointer on his metal address book to C and popped the lid. He ran his finger down the listings, then dialed Robert's home number.

"Mrs. Cooper? Mitch Antree here. I'm doing splendidly, thank you, how about yourself? Almost feels like spring, doesn't it? Well, I did have one thing. I asked Robert if he'd be able to work late tonight, and he expressed some concern as to whether that would be all right with you. Uh-huh. Well, I'm afraid it might be very late indeed. We've got a very significant client in town that we need to have dinner and discussions with, and I expect it will be, oh, round about midnight before Robert gets home." Antree winked at Maurice, who made a face. "Oh yes, I wouldn't ask if it weren't important. No, I'll see to it that he gets a good supper. Why, thank you, Mrs. Cooper. The same to you."

He hung up and smiled at Robert. "Any other questions?"

He was full of them. Was it safe? Would no one care that he was white? But stronger still was the desire to cross the line, to see for himself.

"No," Robert said. "No more questions."

At six they all got into Antree's Cadillac, with its factory air conditioning, leather seats, and 396-cubic-inch V8. Robert hung back slightly to see how the seating arrangements would fall out, and wasn't terribly surprised to see Maurice automatically take the front passenger seat.

They were in Hayti in five minutes. Antree idled on Pettigrew Street outside the Wonderland Theater while Maurice ran up to the box office to get tickets. Robert tried not to stare. Close as it was to the office, Robert had never been there on a weekend. Part of it could have been guilt. If things went the way Antree claimed they would, Robert would be building the East-West Freeway right through the middle of the neighborhood.

In northwest Durham, where Robert lived, a few of his neighbors might sit out on their porches for an evening, cigarettes and citronella candles burning against the mosquitoes, while everyone else hurried inside to their televisions. Here the entire neighborhood seemed to be on the sidewalk.

It was like the stories Robert had heard about street corners in Harlem. Negro businessmen in suits stopped to shake each other's hands. Women wore skirts slit nearly to the waist, and blouses cut for maximum provocation. There were Negro GIs from Camp Butner, tightly creased and standing in clumps, school kids in striped T-shirts and bright jackets, old men with suspenders and canes and snap-brim fedoras.

Maurice got in the car and Antree edged into the traffic, crawling east to Fayetteville Street, where he found an open spot at the curb and parked.

"I suppose we're going to Elvira's," Maurice said.

"That Jake with you?" Antree said.

"I expect I can take it if Robert can. How's your tolerance for grease, Robert?"

"Compared to what I get at home," Robert said, "I'm sure it'll be fine."

They locked the car and Robert found himself swimming upstream through a river of black humanity. Along with the crowd came the sound, a chorus that rose and fell in slow waves, peaking when three or four voices surfaced momentarily into audible words, then fading again below the rattle of broken mufflers, the drumming of high heels on concrete, the chirp and whistle of distant radios, the claps and hoots and laughter and surprise.

It was impossible not to brush up against strange Negro bodies. Robert quickly got over his first shock and found nothing to be afraid of. No one seemed to pay him particular attention. I'm handling this well, he thought.

A couple of the storefronts along Fayetteville Street were boarded up, but when they turned the corner onto Pettigrew, business seemed good. They could hear the presses working inside Service Printing on the corner, and the Carolina Times next door was bustling. Next to Pee Wee's Shoe Shop was a big plate-glass window that read *Elvira's Club Dine-Et*. It was part of a contiguous block of storefronts whose second floors sat back a good ten feet from the first. Peeling white paint covered the bricks as high as the tops of the doors and windows, with plain red brick above.

"So what gives, here?" Robert said. "This place doesn't look like a slum to me."

"Keep your voice down, won't you?" Maurice said. "Some folks around here are not that crazy about the word *slum* these days."

Robert felt his face heat up. "Sorry. You know what I mean. This isn't what I expected."

"Not enough winos in the doorways for you?" Maurice asked. "They'll be out later, never fear."

"I said I was sorry."

"It was different here, even five years ago," Maurice said. "Better. It was only when all this renewal talk started up that everybody gave up trying. Why put glass in that broken window when the appraisers are going to pay you the same for cardboard?"

Through the screen doors of the restaurant wafted smells of burning fat, yeast, cornbread, collards, and spilled beer.

"We can talk inside," Antree said, rubbing his hands. "I need me some soul food."

With one foot in the doorway, Robert had a sudden memory of the stories his father had read to him as a child. It was possible to come and go from Fairyland as long as you followed a few simple rules: Don't pick up any stray objects, don't make any wagers with magical beings, that sort of thing. Above all, never eat the food. Once you'd eaten their food, they had you forever.

For all its shabbiness, Hayti seemed a magical place. As he crossed Elvira's threshold he thought, What would it be like to belong here?

In the end the food was neither unpalatable nor particularly exotic. They all had fresh chicken fried in grease that was not so fresh, collard greens with bits of dried ham, white corn, and sweet potato pie. Afterward, Maurice accepted a Lucky, and he and Robert smoked while Antree drank a third beer.

Robert's feelings were complex. He'd been married for two years now, and a fulltime employee for just as long. He had found moments of contentment standing in the morning mist and looking at his house, his lawn, his quiet street. There was still pleasure, on rare occasions, in bed with Ruth. Work alternately absorbed and bored him, and the excitement of rebuilding Hayti and creating the East-West Freeway seemed to recede constantly into the future.

He hadn't been to see live music since college. The idea of it stirred something in him, memories and longings, a sense of formless possibility, a tang of the forbidden. The libertine atmosphere of Hayti magnified the risks—not only the physical danger that lurked there, but the loss of control that beckoned from darkened doorways. It was, Robert thought, something like Havana before the revolution, a place where you checked your inhibitions at the door.

"Shall we?" Maurice asked, pushing back his chair.

"Yeah, man," Antree said. Robert felt like a teenager, dizzy with anticipation.

The Wonderland Theater was two blocks east, between Elvira's and the Biltmore Hotel. It was a three-story red brick cube, with a wide arch across the front that rose as high as the second story windows on either side. The words *Wonderland Theater* were cut into the stone of the arch and the box office nestled neatly inside the recess. The place still served as a theater, and glass frames held posters for *The Great Escape* and *Fun in Acapulco*.

A crowd had already formed, with an hour yet until showtime. Robert couldn't remember ever being among so many black people in such close proximity. The truth, he saw, was that he was at one end of a spectrum of skin colors, many of them no darker than his own. The crowd was mostly male, mostly in coats and ties, though there were some turtlenecks and open sport shirts. The main thing that struck him was the obvious care and effort that virtually every one of them had spent on his appearance: hats, slickly processed hair, brightly shined shoes, rings, cufflinks, tie tacks.

Then there were the women. Some wore furs and broad-brimmed hats, others simple linen dresses and dime-store gloves. They had an ease with their own bodies, no matter what size or shape, that Robert found both alien and appealing. And some of them were simply stunning. He was unable to stop looking at one woman whose long, white silk dress clung to her hourglass figure as if static electricity was all that held it on. She had curly black hair past her shoulders, creamy tan skin, olive colored eyes, delicate features, and a half smile that made her seem oblivious to everyone around her, as if she were turned inward to focus on the soft hum of the biological machinery that moved her so gracefully through the crowd.

They began to file into the lobby. The slightly threadbare, multicolored carpet there held the smell of popcorn, though at the moment the concession stand was serving liquor.

"You want something?" Antree asked. Robert shook his head, thinking he should keep his wits about him. Antree waded away through the crowd. Maurice didn't seem inclined to conversation. He was nodding slightly as people caught his eye, smiling occasionally. Robert put his hands in his pockets and tried in vain to look inconspicuous.

Antree came up behind him with two glass tumblers. "The only scotch they had was J&B, that all right?"

"You're buying, I'm not complaining," Maurice said.

"Look who I ran into at the bar," Antree said, and Robert turned around to find himself face to face with the woman in the white dress.

"Hi," he said, thinking fast. "I'm Robert."

She raised one eyebrow and let him take her hand, which she offered with fingers down and wrist bent. "Charmed, I'm sure," she said. She was not as tall as he'd thought at first. Her perfume was delicate, sweet, intoxicating.

"Barrett, how're you doing?" Maurice asked, reaching past Robert to shake the hand of someone standing next to the woman in white.

"Maurice. What you know good?" the man said.

Antree said, "Barrett Howard, this is Robert Cooper, my new engineer."

Robert forced himself to look away from the woman long enough to shake Howard's hand. The man's grip made a statement, Robert discovered. The statement was, "I can take you." He was six feet tall and looked like he lifted weights. His hair was unprocessed and grown out unevenly half an inch or more. His broad, dark face looked too young for the number of lines crisscrossing it. He wore a blue dress shirt, open at the throat, with a thin black tie hanging loose and a navy blue blazer on top. His pants were dark khaki, worn over suede cowboy boots with pointed toes. "Hey there," he said.

Robert had seen Howard's face on the evening news. "He looks like a gorilla," Ruth had said, and Robert had let the racist implications pass at the time. Newspaper and TV commentators portrayed him as a kind of monster, violent and threatening in an almost sexual way, not just an integrationist but a Communist and a revolutionary. Randy Fogg, on WRAL radio, regularly referred to him as "Fidel" Howard, "The Red Negro," "The Black Stalin," and a dozen other epithets. Yet here he was, shaking Robert's hand.

"Nice to meet you," Robert said, then hated himself for the banality. Before he could redeem himself, Antree had his arm around Howard's shoulder.

"You going to talk tonight?" Antree asked.

"Nah, man, I'm here to listen to the music, like everybody else. Listen, I got to go."

"I can dig it," Antree said. "You be cool, now."

Howard nodded distractedly, scooped the woman up by her narrow waist, and pushed into the crowd.

"Who is she?" Robert asked.

Maurice looked at Antree. "Now see what you've done?"

"Don't even think about her," Antree said. "Don't even look."

"What's her name?" Robert asked.

"Trouble," Antree said. "Capital T."

"I know who Barrett Howard is," Robert said.

"I'm not talking about Barrett Howard," Antree said. "Forget that crap you see on TV. Howard's a pussycat. She's the one you have to watch out for."

Robert looked at him blankly.

"You know what a mambo is?" Antree asked.

"Sure. Perez Prado, 'Cherry Pink and Apple —'"

"No, man, I ain't talking about some Cuban jive. Tell him, Maurice."

Maurice cleared his throat. "The rumor has it that she's a voodoo practitioner. A mambo. Did you see her earrings?"

Antree said, "I think he might have noticed a necklace, if it hung low enough."

"What earrings?" Robert said.

"Those little heart-shaped things?" Maurice said. "That's hoodoo stuff. Same as on top of St. Joseph's church." He watched Robert's face. "You've never looked at what's on top of St. Joseph's church, have you?"

"You mean the cross?"

"Look again, daddy-o," Antree said. "That ain't no cross."

It felt to Robert like the first few weeks of junior high, when the older boys had mocked him for his ignorance of sex. He hadn't wanted to know what they were taking about, didn't care about the mystery. He wanted them to leave him alone. "Tell me her name," Robert said.

"Mercy," Maurice said. "Her name is Mercy. And if you have any sense at all, you'll leave it at that."

At 8:15 the double doors opened and the crowd made its way down the aisles. The seats had curved wooden backs and red velvet cushions, many of them loose. Robert could not have cared less. In the muted glow of the footlights he saw a black grand piano, a small trap set, a few microphone stands adjusted to varying heights. It was like the first sight of the ocean in summer.

They found seats in the tenth row. Though the show was not scheduled to start until nine, the room was filling quickly. Everyone seemed to know everyone else, as if Robert had crashed a private party of a thousand or so. Men stretched across rows to shake hands, women leaned over the railing of the balcony and shouted through cupped hands. Even Antree was getting into the act, calling out to people in the aisles, while Maurice slid ever lower in his seat, staring at his own knees.

After a few minutes Robert began to feel invisible, began to accept that no one was about to evict him or demand an explanation, and he was able to sit and smoke and observe. He watched Barrett Howard and the woman, Mercy, sail through the crowd like royalty, never lingering with any one group, finally landing on the front row. Everything was foreign, exotic, from the slang that, at its fastest, Robert found incomprehensible, to outsize gestures that were more like dance than anything in Robert's white world of economical movement.

And then, at last, the lights came down and from the darkened stage a man's voice said, "Ladies and gentlemen, welcome to Wonderland," drawing out the ends of the words, "where later tonight Durham's own native son is gonna cool this joint, and you know I got to be talking about Mr. Charlie Shavers and his horn of plenty. But first, from North Carolina College, let's y'all give a warm Wonderland welcome to the Manny . . . Jackson . . . Quartet!"

In the darkness another voice counted to two and then, twice as fast, to four, and the ride cymbal and standup bass took off in a breakneck shuffle. A single, dissonant piano chord broke over the rhythm section like an egg into a hot skillet, and then the lights came up and the tenor sax rode in fast and loose.

Jackson's quartet played for close to an hour. During intermission Antree went for more drinks and Robert sat in a state of quiet euphoria. Then the Shavers quintet took the stage.

Shavers himself was short and thickset, with hair cut so close and jowls so big his head was pear-shaped. He had a pencil-thin mustache and charcoal gray suit and seemed to vibrate like a kettle on full boil, an impression borne out when he would lean back and point his trumpet straight up into the air and unleash a high-pitched squeal of pure joy.

What Robert was beginning to understand was that everything he had painstakingly figured out as he listened to his favorite records, the concepts of harmony and modality and counterpoint, all those ideas were not only true and correct, but in the live, red heat of the moment they were so obvious as to be inconsequential, no more important than Shavers's clowning on stage. All that counted were the pure emotions that the musicians were transmitting from their guts into Robert's.

When the last encore was over, standing in a knot of people outside the Wonderland, Robert knew that he had been transformed, the way heat and pressure turned dull gray shale into glittering mica schist. Secrets he could never put into words had been revealed to him. Some in the audience had heard them and many had not.

Antree, for one, had been largely unaffected. He stood talking to Barrett Howard, and Robert saw that Howard, too, had not been particularly moved. Maurice had. He and Robert looked at each other with the eyes of initiates and nodded and smiled. And Mercy, the woman in white, seemed to float as she walked up to them. Her face perfectly mirrored Robert's own emotions, and she acknowledged it with a radiant smile. As if in a dream, Robert felt her slip into his arms and rest her head against his chest for a heartbeat, then two. He didn't react other than to bring his right hand up and rest it below her shoulder blade, as if they were slow dancing. She was fully present in his arms. He could feel the pressure of her breasts and the heat of her breath through his shirt, smell the aromatic oils in her hair. Then she slipped away again and turned in a slow, elliptical orbit around Howard, lost to everything except the inner worlds the music had opened in her.

"Did that just happen?" Robert asked.

"No," Maurice said. "It most definitely did not happen."

They drifted leisurely down the street, still part of the concert crowd, Antree basking in Howard's attention, Robert tinglingly aware of Mercy as she took her own erratic course around and through them.

The crowd slowly melted away until the three of them were alone on the street next to Antree's Cadillac.

"Well, Maurice?" Antree said. "How's our boy?"

"He's fine. Let's go home."

Robert looked at his distorted reflection in the window of Antree's car. He was not, in fact, fine. He had eaten the food and heard the music, and he was lost.

LEWIS SHINER's books include *Dark Tangos, Black & White, Say Goodbye*, the award-winning *Glimpses*, and *Collected Stories*. All of his work is available for free download at www.fictionliberationfront.net or in print from Subterranean Press.

Street Scenes

My Park, Everybody's Park

CLIFF BELLAMY

ON MAY 14, 2011, during a weekend deluge, a portion of the roof on the southern side of Liberty Warehouse collapsed, flooding the offices of the Liberty Arts metal casting space and other tenants. The city already had condemned portions of the historic tobacco auction house because of roof problems, but the hole in the roof finally forced Liberty Arts, the Scrap Exchange, along with other businesses and nonprofit groups that rented space in the warehouse, to go elsewhere.

More than a year later, the roof of the warehouse still has a big hole where the rain came crashing through. The city-county planning department has implemented demolition-by-neglect proceedings against the landlord-developer that owns the building. The landlord has to fix a number of items soon.

The debate about what will happen to this building, considered the last tobacco auction house still standing in North Carolina, is quintessentially a Durham story—one in which good intentions, a do-it-yourself ethic, and competing visions of downtown redevelopment clash.

If Liberty Warehouse was not located between Foster Street and Rigsbee Avenue, it might be yet another historic structure that has seen better days and is due for the wrecking ball—a sad outcome, but one prompting little real interest or debate. This warehouse is in the heart of Durham Central Park, a part of the city that now has a thriving farmers' market, a skateboard park, the stage and sitting area called the Leaf, and nearby, Motorco Music Hall, Fullsteam Brewery, and other fairly recent arrivals.

Durham Central Park has become the preferred gathering place in the Bull City. It was not always such a welcoming spot. I came to Durham in 1988 to take a job as a copy editor on the *Chapel Hill Herald,* at the time the new edition published by the *Durham Morning Herald* and the *Durham Sun* (now the *Herald-Sun*). The *Herald* at the time was on Market Street, and the copy desk for the Chapel Hill edition worked in the Durham office. I worked a midafternoon-to-later-evening shift and, to save dollars, would park my car north on Foster or Rigsbee or one of the side streets and walk up the hill to the newsroom.

On the advice of colleagues, for the first few months I tried to make the nightly walk back to the car with a buddy or two, after the paper was put to bed. I later became comfortable walking by myself. I think the concerns about crime were exaggerated, but at the time the area's raw, industrial buildings just gave it a menacing aura, at least at night. Suffice it to say, I never dropped by a now-defunct watering hole on Rigsbee Avenue for a nightcap before heading home.

A few years later, the *Herald* (regrettably, but for honorable reasons) left downtown, and I became a member of the newspaper's editorial board. In the mid-1990s, Dr. Curtis Eshelman and other organizers started talking about converting this area around Foster and Rigsbee to a park, one that would become a public space and encourage all kinds of play—athletic and especially artistic.

I thought the organizers had lost their minds. How could this area where people told me to watch my back become a city park, much less a public space where people would feel welcome? The mural that was later painted on the side of a building on Foster Street—showing, among other things, a man playing the cello—seemed like the fantasies of urban utopians.

Today, I am grateful to these utopians.

Part of what I like about Durham is that it's a freak show. I don't mean "freak" in the ugly countercultural sense. Durham freakishness has a nice, generous, giving quality, reflecting a city where people can express themselves in odd ways, without having fingers pointed at them. No place in Durham better symbolizes this freak-flag freedom as Durham Central Park. The park has been the site of a "splash mob" (an organized water fight that a local company put on to allow its employees to let off steam), the Portrait of Durham project (in which people from all over the city met in the park for a group photo that later was featured at the Durham Arts Council), and a parade in honor of a Durham Arts Council exhibit of the work of the late musician Sun Ra. (The Sun Ra-inspired costumes made with castoffs from the Scrap Exchange rivaled Sun Ra's Saturn-inspired garb.) The park is where Tom Whiteside of Durham Cinematheque projects his film collection—sometimes using screens, and often using the sides of buildings—in free summer screenings. The Durham Mardi Gras Parade makes its way up Foster Street and through the park.

When my daughter was younger, we had several birthday parties at the Scrap Exchange, the nonprofit center that encourages re-use of otherwise cast-off items. These parties where my daughter and her friends made their own creations are some of my best memories of her growing up.

A few years ago, I wanted to organize an informal reading honoring Jack Kerouac. When I asked city officials about permits and other logistics, an employee at Parks and Recreation suggested Durham Central Park. As long as no sound system was used, we were free to gather and read in the park without a permit. I posted some fliers, sent some email invitations, and in October 2009 about a dozen people came to the grassy area next to Liberty Warehouse and read some of their favorite passages.

I am very proud of this reading, and gratified by the people who showed up. It could not have happened anywhere but Durham Central Park. A few months ago, almost in tribute to that mural, I took my cello up to the Leaf and played for about a half hour, the whoosh of nearby skateboarders a counterpoint to my efforts to master "Birdland."

None of the parades, readings, and splash mobs would have happened without the efforts of those early dreamers, and the people who first came to Central Park. Those Liberty Warehouse tenants who had to move when the roof collapsed were there when the park's vision first got underway. The Scrap Exchange was one of the first organizations to locate to the warehouse, and it quickly became an anchor for Durham Central Park. Later, private dollars built the George Watts Hill Pavilion for the Arts next to the warehouse. How many cities can boast a public foundry where you can watch artists and craftsmen transform hot metal into shapes? Liberty Arts' metal working demonstrations in the pavilion became attractions in the park. (Liberty Arts still uses the pavilion, which shares a wall with Liberty Warehouse, for occasional demonstrations and pours.)

Later, the city built the farmers' market pavilion, the skate park, and the bridge over the pond south of the warehouse, and soon the park was starting to resemble that mural.

I write about music and the arts for the newspaper. Before the roof collapsed last year I had written about the Scrap Exchange's desire to raise money for a new, permanent space, the Durham Cinematheque summer movies in the park, and the Portrait of Durham project.

The Monday after the roof collapsed, I went to the warehouse and spoke to many of the artists and tenants who were packing up their goods, in anticipation that the city would soon prohibit them from entering the building for safety reasons. That day, the artists who used the warehouse for their work knew the neighborhood would never be the same and were already lamenting the loss of an arts-related community.

Today, many tenants have moved to other spaces. The two anchors, Liberty Arts and the Scrap Exchange, have moved to the Cordoba Building on Franklin Street, and are helping to establish a new arts-related district. There is buzz that the Cordoba Building will carry on the Durham Central Park vision in another location.

The Durham Central Park neighborhood is in transition. No one knows if Liberty Warehouse will be renovated and sold to a developer with bigger plans, or whether it is destined for the wrecking ball (although preservationists have pledged to save the building).

Not long ago, no one would have believed that Durham would build a performing arts center that attracts national artists, or that American Tobacco would be renovated. American Tobacco and the Durham Performing Arts Center are wonderful venues. However, they represent a different idea of downtown than Durham Central Park. If Liberty Warehouse becomes a mirror of American Tobacco, it may be a welcome economic move and put more tax dollars in the city coffers, but the money would come at the expense of changing the character of the park.

At a recent Art Walk, the city closed off Foster Street. On this warm afternoon, people were throwing footballs, riding skateboards, lining up at the food trucks, and cooling out in the Leaf. Liberty Warehouse sits empty, its doors padlocked. Whatever happens to it, I want the park to remain the kind of public gathering place its founders envisioned, the place where you can throw a ball, show films, or play the cello.

CLIFF BELLAMY writes about arts and books for the *Herald-Sun*. He has lived in the Durham area since 1988. He grew up in Wilmington where his family was instrumental in integrating the public schools. He plays cello and likes all kinds of music, but has a passion for the music of Duke Ellington, Miles Davis, and other artists who play America's classical music.

Boom

PAM SPAULDING

1. Boom & Bust

MY POLITICAL BLOG, Pam's House Blend (pamshouseblend.com), covers national news mostly related to lesbian, gay, bisexual, and transgender (LGBT) rights, and politics surrounding gender issues, race, and the religious right. I also sometimes blog about local issues. In 2010, I was asked to write a column for the *Durham News*, which gave me an opportunity to get off the political hamster wheel and focus on the boom and bust of life in the Bull City.

I'm forty-eight—squarely in middle-age territory—still young enough to occasionally wear my hair in ponytails (okay, it may look silly), old enough to struggle with bifocals. As a Bull City native, I've lived long enough to see the composition of the city and the Triangle change enormously.

When I tell people I'm a Durhamite, chances are that, more often than not, they are not from around here, or even the South for that matter. The changing face of the Bull City's population first became clear to me back in the early 1990s, when I returned to the city after I'd lived in New York City (Bed-Stuy Brooklyn, to be exact) for many years. I moved to Old West Durham, the neighborhood adjacent to Duke's East Campus that includes Ninth Street and north to Watts-Hillandale. I joined the neighborhood association. The icebreaker question offered up by president John Schelp at the first neighborhood meeting I attended was, "Who is a native of Durham?" In a room full of people, my hand was the only one to go up.

I always like to ask how long some of the newbies have been in Durham. Many have lived here less than five years, so they really have no idea how much things have changed. Everyone has landmarks and mental bookmarks of their childhood hometown. One I like to share with newcomers takes me back to the mid-Seventies long before the area now known as South Square along Durham–Chapel Hill Boulevard was home to Sam's Club or a SuperTarget. Back then, it was a big empty field with some trees.

One of the few businesses along the boulevard in those years was Mario's, a family-owned Italian restaurant that had genuine New York-style pizza; the owners were native New Yorkers, so it was the real deal. For a kid who spent summers eating pizza in New York while visiting relatives, I considered Mario's a slice (literally) of heaven.

Then in 1975, that land was cleared and the site was transformed into South Square Mall, the city's premier all-interior box mall. Durham was a pretty sleepy town back then (from a twelve-year-old's point of view, anyway), so the mall became a big draw. It was the first mall in the area with four movie theaters and a food court. There was a Belk-Leggett, a JC Penney, and a Piccadilly Cafeteria, among other stores. It drew shoppers from all over the Triangle.

When I moved back to Durham, I would stop by South Square Mall from time to time and see how it was changing. Back when the mall was sparkly and new, it had been a safe haven for kids. But starting in the mid-Eighties into the late Nineties, the two-story traditional mall headed into a serious downward spiral. The movie theaters closed. The place was no longer a safe teen hangout. Increasingly, it had little to offer patrons of any age.

With the announcement of plans to construct a new mall that would be called the Streets at Southpoint on I-40, beleaguered South Square became dead-man-walking. In no time flat, anchor tenants Belk and JC Penney left for the new high-style mall; Dillard's hung around until the plug was pulled on the nearly empty South Square in 2002. At that point, it had become an eyesore, a big, white elephant, occupying a prime piece of real estate. It was a relief to see the wrecking balls finally show up to put the place out of its misery.

It may have been just a mall; but it held a special place in my childhood memories. And now, I'm one of many Americans who can measure my age in mall-years—the number of times I've seen a mall built, decay, die, and be demolished, the boom and bust of twenty-first century life.

2. Film at 11' 8"

FAST-FORWARD PAST THE MALL to the workplace, which in my case is Brightleaf Square, the retail and office complex on Gregson and Main streets downtown. Most people around here know the place. What they don't appreciate are the accompanying sound effects. Enter Jurgen Henn.

I've not sure when I met him. We both work in Brightleaf Square. And like everyone else who works in those two renovated tobacco warehouse buildings, Jurgen and I periodically hear box trucks slam into the nearby railroad bridge at Gregson and Peabody.

The trestle is clearly marked with a sign that says 11' 8" to indicate the clearance, and its supporting iron beam has flashers to alert truck drivers that their rig is too tall. But those precautions don't seem to reduce the frequency of box truck decapitations.

Jurgen Henn decided to turn the accidents into art, a video project. He works in the South Building, where he has a clear view of the bridge.

He set up a camera and captured crash after crash and loaded a compilation of them onto YouTube. It became a sensation.

And the video footage isn't restricted to trucks; there are videos of cars getting into the action, with inattentive drivers rear-ending each other under the bridge.

I've worked in the North Building for fifteen years and have lost count of the number of times I've heard the *boom* of metal scraping metal as the trucks speed down Gregson (usually at a speed that causes pedestrians to jump back onto the curb) and slam into the bridge, getting trapped. Usually this results in the top of the truck being peeled back like a sardine can. More than a few of my Brightleaf co-workers have collected the interesting twisted pieces of metal and hung them on their walls as, well, "found art."

I've actually only witnessed the box truck–car–bridge collisions a couple of times, but I hear them regularly. The most recent crash happened a few months ago while I was getting a cup of tea at Alivia's on Main, which also faces the bridge. The morning conversations were momentarily interrupted by the now-familiar *Boom!* Regulars nonchalantly turned around but kept talking.

Jurgen's box-truck disaster videos provide some laughs and a lot of interest. They've been featured in media outlets from the *Herald-Sun* to *Der Spiegel*. The footage raises the serious issue of speeding down Gregson. Bull City folks want to live in a safe, walkable (and bike-able and drive-able) downtown. In this neighborhood that's still a hit-or-miss proposition—no pun intended. There's work to be done. Until then, Jurgen Henn's office cam will keep on witnessing.

PAM SPAULDING is editor and publisher of the national blog pamshouseblend.com, ranked in the top fifty progressive political blogs, which has been profiled in the *News & Observer*, *Washington Post*, *The New Yorker*, *New York Times*, and the *Advocate*. She is a guest blogger at *Salon* and *Huffington Post*, and has provided political commentary on CNN, Air America, and *The Michelangelo Signorile Show*. Pam and her wife Kate married in Vancouver in 2004. (Jurgen Henn's videos can be seen at http://11foot8.com.)

Harry Potter on Ninth Street

JOHN VALENTINE

THE FIRST TIME HARRY POTTER turned down Club Boulevard and walked up Ninth Street in the late fall of 1998, he went unnoticed.

It wasn't until winter break a few months later that I had a chance to meet him. My daughters were seven and eleven; we were all on vacation, no homework, and a toasty wood stove inviting us to grab our favorite pillows and quilts and curl up for awhile.

Like most families we had a pile of favorite Christmas books we read aloud over and over. But after the holidays, we wanted the same intimacy and timelessness of reading a book together before bedtime.

Harry was already topping the charts in England and the curious title change between British and American versions had caught my attention. We held *Harry Potter and the Sorcerer's Stone* in our hands, while across the Atlantic, families were tucked in around *Harry Potter and the Philosopher's Stone.* Different cover, different title, even a different size, same beloved book.

So began our love affair with the boy wonder that endures today. As a family we eagerly anticipated each new chapter, adventure, each new semester at Hogwarts.

Some of the sweetest perks of being an independent bookseller are the waves of advance reading copies (ARCs) and review galleys we receive from publisher sales representatives. At the Regulator Bookshop we get weekly packages of these advance books that will be released in hardback in the coming months. Publishers hope we will start a buzz and hand-sell (the booksellers' term for personally recommend) their titles and authors that we enjoy. When sales reps visit to tell us about the next season's books, they often bring along suitcases full of treasures. After we've had a chance to read them, we pass along the old ARCs to local schools, libraries, and prisons. Every book finds a good home, especially children's books.

Scholastic Books is Harry's U.S. publisher. Dawn, their mid-Atlantic sales rep when the Potter series first came out, was a generous, children's-book lover from New Jersey who knew her territory; Dawn and I shared an affinity for her two best-selling series: Ann Martin's "Babysitter Club" and R.L. Stine's "Goosebumps." Then she was elevated to the Harry Potter gatekeeper; once a year for seven years she delivered the coveted ARCs of the next Harry Potter book.

Over the years, I began to have some difficulty trying to keep my family in the read-aloud, chapter-a-night routine. So Dawn made sure I had an advance copy for each girl. I also asked for another copy for the daughter of Tom Campbell, my partner of thirty years at the Regulator. There had to be enough Harrys to go around.

By the time Harry Potter was about to launch the third book in the series, my kids grew impatient with my "we need to stop now" rule. They started reading ahead over my shoulder, accusing me of doing the same. Then, inevitably, they would just slide the book out of my hands and disappear into their rooms. Homework would always suffer during Harry Potter weeks.

As word got out that Harry Potter books were actually available before the release date, I started getting wonderful, pleading, scribbled letters from children and parents. Our family's advance copies, once we finished them, went on loan. They became deliciously dog-eared, and were always returned, often with effusive thank-you notes.

There was another way to get a jump on the upcoming Harry Potter. The first three books in the adventure series were published months earlier in Great Britain. Durham had an engaged underground of fans who imported the books.

In the United States, the Harry Potter books were usually released in early summer. The Regulator started having midnight madness parties the night of the book release. One thousand costumed Harrys, Rons, and Hermiones lined Ninth Street. Enthusiastic friends and eager high school students beefed up our staff. We transformed the Regulator's entrance into Platform 9 ¾, as anticipatory fantasy ruled our funky street. Several times local newspaper reporters embedded with us while we prepared the store for midnight's magical assault and mayhem. Neighboring coffee shops and gift stores stayed open later to share the Halloween-like energy.

The night's contained giddy craziness was always entertaining, the line to the front cash register wound hundreds of yards upstairs and down, through every section of the store. My favorite scenes were the children curled up in the bookstore's nooks reading the coveted latest story. Some even brought their favorite pillows. Face painting, quizzes, witches and wizard word puzzles couldn't hold a Hogwarts' candle to J.K. Rowling's delicious tales in print.

It was the same crowd and enthusiasm for days after each Harry launch. As I dropped my daughter off at the Duke University bus stop for Camp Riverlea, a popular local outdoor day camp, children were clutching their Harrys along with backpacks, bathing suits, lunch boxes, and tennis rackets. When I would wave goodbye, I'd see half of her bus mates with their heads down, already reading.

By the fifth book, Harry was so big that marketing became global, corporate, and Muggle-managed. No more advance reading copies; book drop dates, the official worldwide release date stamped in bold on each box, and times were synchronized; and booksellers had to sign three-page affidavits, agreeing that boxes of the new Harry would not even be opened until the official release date. Two days prior, a tractor-trailer arrived at a prescribed time at our back loading dock to deliver shrink-wrapped pallets. Even the packing tape on each box was printed with scary cautions.

The publisher had good cause to resort to such measures. On the night of the release, *empty* boxes of Harry Potter V were selling for five dollars on eBay.

Each midnight event, we would unpack the bright white boxes in the front display area in full view of the crowds lined up on the street. The first fifty people through the door always got souvenir empties.

My daughters weren't always in town for the big release. I cut into our embargoed supply and FedEx'd Harrys all over the U.S. to various summer camps. One year my youngest daughter and wife were driving cross-county. They called from the Tattered Cover, the phenomenal indy bookstore in Colorado, to share the unique wonder of another Harry book launch in a different time zone. They described an equally entertaining Mardi Gras scene. Denver and Durham were as one.

In 2007, for *Harry Potter and the Deathly Hallows,* the seventh installment in the series, my oldest daughter was away at college in New York. I made sure she got her book on time, sending a package clearly labeled with a "Deliver by July 20, 2007. Do not open until July 21, 2007!" warning. She and I had discussed how nervous the publisher was about leaked copies, especially since this was the final book; bloggers everywhere were guessing what was going to happen.

She called twice that night. "Dad is it okay if I go into the city to Barnes & Noble?" she asked. In our house, just mentioning B&N was like saying *Voldemort.* The big-box store was throwing an over-the-top launch, with dozens of costumed characters, events, and giveaways. My daughter, a total fan of the drama and magic everywhere, had to go. Of course I said yes. "But don't take the book! It's not officially out yet." I advised her to take a colorful Scholastic promo goodie book bag with Harry on the cover that the publisher had sent in limited quantities to independent bookstores.

At 12:30 she called again. "Dad, the city is crazy tonight. I just saw a bus-load of Death Eaters on Forty-second Street! And a live owl at the store." She and her friends had planned an invasion that Harry and Hermione would have been proud of.

They had snuck in the book. "It was like our wand, Dad." Empowered New York college girls, each having devoured the first six Harry Potters through their teenage years, they had talked their way past security. "Of course we're on the guest list!" She had waved the magic promo bag while one of her friends carried the precious book secured in a pillow. They said they felt invincible and they had to see that owl.

Such was the power of a new Harry Potter book.

Over the years, Dawn sent me several autographed J.K. Rowling's. She told me stories of friends who held back cartons of advance reading copies to pay for their kids' college education. We shook our heads as the movies rolled out with embarrassing amounts of promo trinkets and merchandise — overpriced pewter bookmarks, cartoon sticker-books, and mini-posters.

Though I do still like my collection of HP lightning bolt logo baseball caps! And that cardboard faux treasure box for the boxed set, not too shabby. Can't forget that bright red special edition Hogwarts electric train set, complete with tunnels and a platform. It's stored in the attic. Somewhere, too, at the ready, is a vintage tuxedo, with a faded purple, iron-on Gryffindor patch.

Harry still shows up at the Regulator; of course he's a rock star now. Every once in a while, I'll hear a parent calling to a child, "Come on sweetie, we have to go." And there the son or daughter will be, curled up in a corner or on the sofa, back in school with Hagrid, Dumbledore, and the Weasleys, chasing the golden egg on a faraway Quidditch pitch.

JOHN VALENTINE is a chief contributor to the *Independent Weekly.* He was an original "Our Lives" columnist in the Raleigh *News & Observer.* He is co-owner of the Regulator Bookshop on Ninth Street in Durham. In 2012, he won a journalism award from the North Carolina Press Association for his Front Porch columns in the *Independent Weekly.*

Open for Business

TORI REYNOLDS

Across the highway from the café
where the lawn is strewn with pink and green
sunglassed boys and girls slung
in Adirondack chairs, balancing
small baskets of baked scones and lattes
on their laps, *Las Mariposas Salon de Belleza*
keeps the neon sign in its tinted window lit,
the white, windowless door, shut.

On Saturdays, the city bus stops in front of the café.
Black-haired girls in skinny jeans file off,
cross the ceaseless river of cars on 15-501.
Like skillful needles, they draw all the boys
in need of haircuts close behind.

TORI REYNOLDS has lived in Durham since 1995. She is a clinical psychologist and poet. Her work has appeared in *Sow's Ear* and *PineSong*. She is the recipient of a Vermont Studio Center residency grant.

Gnawin' on Heaven's Door

CHRIS RHYNE REID

AFTER MUCH CAJOLING and convincing, on a Saturday evening in the spring of 2012, I found myself in Duke Park wearing a rainbow tutu, bright pink knee socks, a tank top proclaiming my love for a dancing beaver, and—of course—a large, sequined, bright blue beaver tail. I paraded. I danced. I handed out candy. I performed in front of hundreds of fellow Durhamites, all in an attempt to raise awareness and funds for the Ellerbe Creek Watershed Association.

The Ellerbe Creek Watershed Association gained official nonprofit status in 1999, when I was still an undergraduate journalism student at UNC-Chapel Hill and unaware of Durham's many charms. Through fundraising, education, and hard manual labor, the association has worked to preserve Ellerbe Creek and its watershed, and now owns over 150 acres of land surrounding the creek. Part of the Neuse River basin, Ellerbe flows more than twenty miles through Durham County. It is also home to a wide variety of wildlife, including a large, active beaver lodge.

These beavers are the inspiration for the city's annual Beaver Queen Pageant.

When I try to explain my love for the Bull City to sometimes-skeptical nonbelievers, I often cite the Beaver Queen Pageant, along with some of the city's other quirky events like the Marry Durham celebration, LUEWWD bouts (the League of Upper Extremity Wrestling Women of Durham—yep, that exists), or the Luchadoras women's Mexican wrestling matches.

Sure, it's impossible not to tout the city's thriving culinary scene (from food trucks to fine dining), the passion of Durham residents (from the social activism to the unwavering entrepreneurship), and the arts (from world-class culture to a thriving local music community). I enthusiastically sing the praises of quarry swims, American Tobacco Trail rides, Bulls games, and Eno hikes. But truth be told, at the heart of my love for this city—and the reason I spend a good portion of my days working to help promote it—are its truly unusual events like the Beaver Queen Pageant, events that force you to shrug your shoulders, chuckle a bit, and proclaim with some pride, "Only in Durham."

Years ago, when I agreed to tag along with a friend to check out my first Beaver Queen Pageant, I had no idea what I was in for. Blanket in hand, I was greeted by a park full of hundreds of frolicking Durhamites of all ages in various states of costume, most of whom were wearing some form of homemade beaver tail—large aluminum-foil tails, hand-quilted tails with elaborate stitching, glitter-covered tails, tails made of duct tape and cardboard—even the beloved Bulls' mascot Wool E. Bull was rocking a fuzzy, fur tail.

A ragtag band was playing off to one side of the stage. Families happily picnicked, folks threw Frisbees, kids bounced from the playground to the kiddie pool, and bottles of wine and appetizing nibbles were passed around. A couple in their seventies danced cozily in front of our chosen spot, and a friendly collie made himself comfortable on our blanket. Enthusiastic

179

neighbors who lived in a large, white house across from the park offered up cocktails made with homemade tonic to anyone who strolled by and was willing to toss the residents' chosen beaver queen candidate a vote.

Another unique Durham institution, the Scrap Exchange, set up a booth during the pageant and provided materials so tail-less audience members could correct that deficiency if so inspired.

Started by a group of neighbors, who now call themselves the Beaver Lodge Local 1504, the Beaver Queen Pageant is held each spring when the Southern heat hasn't become miserably unbearable and the mosquitoes haven't quite begun their hunt for blood. It's a fundraiser but also a tongue-in-cheek competition where contestants (both men and women) wearing elaborate beaver-themed costumes vie to be crowned Durham's official beaver queen. In addition to the crown, contestants compete for Best Tail, Best Stage Presence, Best Bribes, Best Talent, and Miss Hygeniality. The festivities are rounded out with live music (usually involving classic rock covers amended to be beaver-themed like "Gnawin' on Heaven's Door" or "I Can't Get No Beaver Action"), food trucks, enough pageantry to satisfy Bert Parks, and—as one would guess—lots of blush-inducing double entendres.

Organizers choose an overall pageant theme; past years' themes have included *The Wild Wild Wetlands, Woodstick,* and *Streampunk.* As frivolous as it sounds, competing to be Durham's Beaver Queen is not for the feint of heart. It requires detailed planning, boundless creativity, and lots of energy. Contestants spend weeks developing their beaver personas, campaigning around town for sponsors, and recruiting friends to be a part of their entourages (friends who are then expected to act as a posse during the pageant, soliciting votes from the crowd and currying favor with the judges).

The festivities kick off with a parade of the contestants and the singing of the official beaver chant, led by the reigning queen. Contestants, their entourages, and audience members stand and sing:

Beaver two, beaver one,
Let's all have some beaver fun!
Beaver four, beaver three,
Let's climb up the beaver tree.

. . . and so on. There is a blessing of the young (aka the kits) where Reverend Morningwood (yep) reads from his fur-covered bible admonishing the little ones to be respectful of beavers and their habitat. Then the competition begins.

The actual competition involves six or so candidates. Dirty as it is, judges pay to participate and are readily bribed with gifts of homemade baked goods, beer and wine (or stronger), favors, fanning, adoration, and cash (all donated to the cause). The beaver queen contestants are judged on their wetlands readywear (a beaver version of swimwear), talent (singing, dancing, science experiments, anything goes), stage presence, quality of tails (size, shape, creativity, functionality), and formalwear (done beaver-style, of course).

Former beaver queens (though it could be argued once a beaver queen, always a beaver queen) include Beaverly Woody, June Cleaver Beaver, Yogi Beaver, and Fabulous Fishscenta Beaver. In 2011, we watched as Scarlet O'Beava, a crowd favorite in 2010 for her curtain-rod dress (an ode to the famed Carol Burnett skit), turned over her crown to Fur Pelton John. Outfitted in gold lamé skintight pants, matching gold metallic boots, and a floor-length, blue-velvet bedazzled coat, Fur Pelton John beat out his rival Cherry Cherry Bang Bang and her twenty-foot beaver tail after he wheeled out a grand piano constructed entirely out of cardboard during the talent competition.

The most recent pageant featured a circus theme and contestants included Furrah Gnawsett-Major (married to Durham's iconic Major the Bull), Down Under Beaver, Bailar Beaver, Dr. Jekyll & Mrs. Beaver, Marilyn DamHo, and Taco Belle. Furrah Gnawsett-Major easily secured her victory and brought the entire crowd to its feet after the talent competition when she quietly walked on stage in purple polyester bell-bottom pants and a feathered neon-green wig, and proceeded to play the entire *Star Wars* theme on the clarinet while hula-hooping—yes, hula-hooping without missing a beat. She scored bonus points for being joined on stage by two pint-size kids dressed up as mini beaver-tailed versions of Princess Leia and Luke Skywalker.

I have a friend in Chapel Hill who argues that there are just one thousand like-minded individuals in Durham who love nothing more than dressing up in costumes and celebrating, all the while raising money for one charity or another. I admit, we Durhamites unabashedly love to find a reason for a shindig and a cause to rally around. What's wrong with that? We Durham residents, while fighting the good fight, don't take ourselves too seriously and, like the Beaver Queen Pageant itself, never shy away from a little tail shaking.

As Friends of the Ellerbe say, *PEACE, LOVE, BEAVER!* Long live the queen, long live the creek.

CHRIS RHYNE REID is a copywriter by day and is one of the voices behind the popular Durham website, Carpe Durham, where parts of this piece originally appeared. She was honored to be a part of Bailar Beaver's team in 2012.

Homeward

Best of Towns, Worst of Towns
—My Town

KATY MUNGER

EVERY YEAR, in a goofy tradition that I find both charming and a little strange, hundreds of residents step forward to marry Durham, filling a downtown square with their vows to love my town until "death does us part." I've never had the slightest inclination to join in this public display of affection. But only recently have I come to understand why: I don't want to marry Durham for the same reason I don't want to marry anyone. Like every other relationship I have ever had, I fight my love for Durham when I'm in it, and miss it when I'm away from it. In short, Durham is my ultimate love/hate relationship.

It's an odd pull, considering that I moved here for the same reason I get involved in a lot of relationships — it reminded me of a younger time. I had grown up in Raleigh, lived in New York City for much of my adult life, and then decided to move back to North Carolina in 1996. By then, Raleigh had changed, much like an old friend with a facelift gone awry. The same basic structure was there but it had a completely different overlay. It disconcerted me. The capital city seemed like the Home Shopping Network come alive, instead of the iconoclastic Southern town I remembered. I felt far more at home in Durham, mostly because it reminded me of Raleigh during my growing-up years — gritty, creative, and blessedly blue collar, yet academic at the same time. Best of all, it was as diverse as the Big Apple I had just left behind and I found that I needed that diversity to feel as if I were still in the real world.

Discovering Durham was a coming home present. Until then, my only memory of the Bull City dated back to the mid-Sixties when my fourth grade class rode in a rickety old school bus down Highway 70 to visit the Liggett & Myers cigarette factory in downtown Durham. Not only was it still okay for people to smoke back then, when we left the factory our tour guide presented each of us with a gigantic cigarette a good two feet long that had failed to be properly trimmed by the cutting machine. All the way home, my classmates and I pretended to smoke our ultra-ultra-ultra-longs. For decades, this experience shaped my view of Durham: the rich smell of tobacco, a bumpy bus ride, brick warehouses, and wiry old men with grizzled faces.

Yet here I was, thirty years later, so in love with Durham that I only dated it for a few weeks before I moved in — lock, stock, and barrel — buying a big house in Forest Hills. There I might have stayed forever. But, as usually happens whenever one of my relationships stabilizes, I found that I was bored. The unknown began calling to me. It started when I realized that there, right behind the lovely houses of Beverly Drive, separated by a broken bridge that fittingly went nowhere, was one of the Durham's poorest neighborhoods. Its cinderblock homes and weary-looking residents reminded me of the Caribbean. It fascinated me. I began to test my self-imposed boundaries, driving through neighborhoods where I looked jarringly out of place in my Sebring convertible. I inched my way down side streets off Holloway and Angier, drawing stares and looks of incredulity from the residents. I had no business being there and they knew it.

Although I did not know it at the time, I wanted to understand Durham. I knew I had to leave my comfort zone to do that. I think, too, that I was homesick for New York. I began driving further and further from home. Once, I discovered a block that rivaled the ravaged streets of Bedford-Stuyvesant — only to find it was bordered by a perfect gem of a neighborhood filled with brightly painted clapboard houses and land-scaped yards right out of a fairy tale. I searched the faces of the strangers I passed, wondering who they were, what they had once wanted out of life, what they still wanted, and why none of my neighbors ever talked about the existence of the poorer neighborhoods I had seen. There were two Dur-hams living parallel to each other, it seemed, and neither Durham wanted to cross the divide.

189

As the years sped by, the dichotomy of Durham continued to fascinate me. How could a town that had wrapped itself around the golden granite towers of Duke University also contain such poverty and deprivation? The enigma drew me in, its contradictions blinding me to the obvious: Durham was that way because enough people in power kept it that way. I learned this during my brief but eventful career in grassroots politics. I plunged into it, full of optimism, much as I begin all my relationships. But just as you eventually have to face the fact that you can't change a significant other, you cannot change a town. At least not on your own.

I fled Durham politics a few years later, not so much bruised as sad-dened to learn that there are people in this world willing to fight change simply so they can cling to their meager power. I could accept the existence of poverty as part of human existence. But to realize that people could do something about it, and chose not to, broke my heart. It took a long time for me to swallow that dose of reality.

I had to withdraw. For a while, my slice of Durham was little bigger than a modest home in a middle-class neighborhood near Duke's West Campus. I went about the business of being a single mom and told myself I was busy enough with family, my nonprofit job, and my crime fiction writing, all of which, god knows, was true. But I was still dealing with the fact that my funky, beloved hometown had an ugly side and that, like all things in life, it was less than perfect. Disillusionment can be a terrible thing when you're a born optimist.

Eventually, the siren song of Durham began to call to me again. Life goes on. This time, I've been cautious with my love. I revel in St. Patrick's Day at the James Joyce Pub and pay good money for tickets to DPAC, where I always am pleasantly surprised to discover that the sightlines and acoustics are better than anything Broadway has ever offered me. I've come to love playing darts at the Green Room, eating homemade tamales from the cow store near my house, and watching concerts on Friday nights at the American Tobacco Campus.

Summer evenings at the Durham Bulls stadium have become as comfortable as hanging out at home, one of the few places on earth where I can let myself have more than one beer and watch as my To Do list floats away over the infield into the night. I am a frequent observer of Sunday brunches at Motorco, ordering Bloody Marys served with olives and bacon, and sipping them under spinning ceiling fans while sunlight pours through the picture windows and children of all ages frolic on the dance floor to gospel funk.

I have even learned to affectionately tolerate Durham's innumerous thirty-something hipsters, even though I am rapidly approaching the age at which anyone younger than me is inherently annoying. They are undeniably intelligent and good-hearted. All those mutts they squire around town prove it: Durhamites do love their rescue dogs. Most of all, this new breed of foodie-meets-social-activist is building a modern personality for Durham that breaks with the past. I love seeing my town become some place new: Soho-meets-Main-Street and it works.

Eventually, as is the case with all lasting relationships, I have come to love Durham for what it is, not for what I want it to be. Yes, there is something raw and painful about how my town, more than many towns, wears its haves and have-nots out in the open. But it is the real world and doesn't pretend otherwise. Thus it is that I still proudly call myself a citizen of Durham—the town that is what it is, with few pretensions; the town that manages to find room for everyone, without making anyone feel out of place; the town that, like all good relationships, lets you be yourself.

KATY MUNGER is a crime fiction writer with fourteen novels published to date, including the Casey Jones series. Two of the Casey Jones titles, *Money to Burn* and *Better Off Dead*, explore the unique social personality of Durham. Her most recent book is *Angel of Darkness*. A founding member of the Tart Noir genre, she was a reviewer for the *Washington Post's* now-defunct book section, and is an original member of Thalia Press Author Co-op. She is also Outreach Director for Progress North Carolina. Her website is katymunger.com.

Watermark

CEIL CLEVELAND

"DURHAM! WHY IN THE WORLD would you want to move to Durham?" spluttered the man with whom I had shaken hands at a party in Chapel Hill. His implication, I assume, was that any enlightened couple moving from New York would naturally light in Chapel Hill. I had a lame answer for him then, something about finding a house that worked for us in a beautiful setting. Even then, in 2004, I knew enough about my new home to feel insulted by his view of our bad judgment or poor taste or both. With enough Pinot Grigio, I managed to enjoy the rest of the evening.

After eight years here, I have learned a good deal more, and have taken an informal poll of my family, who live in New York, Ohio, Texas, and Washington State, but who often visit.

"It's the theatre, culture, music, documentary film festival" (our actor/director/musician/film producer family says, after visiting DPAC, Carolina Theatre, Common Ground, Manbites Dog).

"It's the art" (our artist/set designer family says, after visiting the Nasher, Storefront Project, Art Walks).

"It's Cameron Indoor Stadium, Duke programs, the nearness of other universities" (my husband, sons, Duke alum family say, after many blue-faced games, irrational shouting, rational lectures, tent cities).

"It's the books and readings" (my bookworm family says, after visiting the Regulator, Books Do Furnish a Room, and Eno River Unitarian Universalist book sales).

"It's the fabulous restaurants, Brightleaf Square, farmers' market" (the foodies in our family say, after visiting these and Four Square, Nana's, Rue Cler, Watts Grocery, Revolution, Broad Street Cafe, when our favorite jazz group plays).

"It's Occupy Durham, and the hysterical stiff-legged, mantra-spouting, consumer-mocking Zombie Shoppers at Southpoint Mall on Black Friday, 'Kids see Zombie, kids smile. Zombie no disrupt. Zombie no have ID; Zombie dead'" (my activist/comedian family says).

But they are just plain nuts. Who cares about culture, art, music, books, sports, intellectual stimulation, food, activist humor? What a crock!

"It's the water, stupid" (says the matriarch of this large, opinionated, multitalented blended family—five children, four spouses, five grandchildren). My Maslow pyramid of needs is just a little different, is all. And you out there, you think Durham is not splashing with fountains of frothing water? Water to live on; water to see every day? That's because you out there didn't look as hard as I did. That's because you never found my special place. My very own sweet spot.

My husband and I, both writers, had managed for our thirty-five years in New York to live on the water—both the Hudson River and an inlet that feeds into Long Island Sound. When we decided to move, we were set on living in Hillsborough among writer friends. But our search led us only to properties too large or too small, and none of them on water. So, try Chapel Hill; that's close: same result. We needed space for two writers and our large, often-visiting family. But, in our sixties, we didn't need a lot of acreage or house to maintain.

I did need water though and vowed not to move anywhere without it. Water to live on. Water to see every day.

Not that this matriarch is stubborn. Just ask my husband and large, opinionated family. Not stubborn, merely obsessed.

All obsessions have a backstory. Here's mine: I had a water-deprived childhood. I grew up on the West Texas High Plains and, as a girl in the Fifties, witnessed a drought of dreadful proportions that parched the land, starved the thirsty black Angus, and drove my rancher father from the cattle business for many years. The closest thing to water I saw was a square, concrete stock tank on the ranch, which in rare non-drought seasons our parents would let us drain, scrub with brushes, and refill to paddle around in. Its depth was such that water never rose above our waists.

I loved the open range, the horses, and the people, but the symbol of my native ground became, for me, the mesquite. Tumbleweeds flourished on our plains, whipping though the fields, attaching themselves to our door and window screens with their prickly fingers when the winds and sand storms got up, as they did in every season but summer. Then they lay scorched and still. My earliest tactile memories are of the gritty diapers my mother attached to me. They left the washer gleaming; then after an hour on the clothesline, they turned the color and texture of sandpaper.

That was in spring. In the winter, the diapers became frozen white squares, which Mother stacked like a pile of pale waffles on a bench in front of the fireplace until they thawed and grew limp as flour tortillas.

In summer, the diapers came off the line so hot you couldn't fold them. Inside, she would stick them in the fridge to cool before she pinned one on a kid. The temperature could crawl to 116 degrees. The absence of water created a mother of invention. Once, when the sheriff threatened to arrest people with the temerity to sprinkle their lawns, my mother ran a hose from the upstairs bathtub, out the window, down the side of the house, and into the front yard, where the runoff from the family bathwater kept the pink crape myrtle blooming feebly. It was the one spot of color in the area, if you didn't count the lone red traffic light blinking night and day as it swung in the wind at the intersection of Main and Center streets.

Today, my mother might get an environmental award for Going Totally Green (or arrested by the sheriff for allowing us to shower too often), but as a teenager, I was Totally Embarrassed by the tube snaking down the side of the house and protested to my heartless mother that I'd never get a boy-friend if she made me live in a house that was taking a perpetual enema.

Until I was twenty-two, I thought life was wind and sand. I thought women's faces by age thirty were *supposed* to look like the bottoms of the dry, cracked, and fissured creek beds that ran through the pastures. I thought that everyone spent each spring in a smelly cellar clinging to their favorite possessions hastily collected, waiting for the spiral above to flatten their houses.

My thirst for water has brought me to this obsessive state. I improbably found a house in Durham that sits on a lovely lake, surrounded by trees that are Totally Green in most seasons. In fall, they are Improbably Golden and scatter their leaves into my lake. Each evening, from our west-facing porch, we see a different natural work of art, a capricious sunset shedding its reflection on our own lake. I do not see the ships and barges I saw from my window on the Hudson. Nor do I see the egrets furled like umbrellas, numinous and mystical, hanging in trees, or the flotilla of swans I saw each day on my Long Island water home. But I do watch my herons and marvel at how they can stand so long on one spindly leg. And I found a turtle, two feet in circumference, under my mailbox.

I have much of my beloved wildlife here—chitters and honks and celestial squawks, ducks, and geese (who leave gifts on my lawn, but hey! they were here before I was), and a robin who made a nest and raised three little blue eggs to birdlets in a holiday wreath I left too long on my door. Even sunsets are almost as splendid as those in Texas. And when we sit on our screened porch enveloped by rain splashing down as it sometimes does, we thrive in a numinous and mystical world of our own, sheltered from the grackling world.

I see and smell water every day. Once, on Mother's Day when I was feeling sorry for myself because none of my far-flung, opinionated children was here to celebrate my being and life-giving talents, our across-the-lake neighbor came gliding toward us in his boat with its rainbow sail that makes me smile every morning when I see it—the boat filled with red, pink, yellow, white roses he had grown. All just for me, the neglected one.

Besides finding neighbors who bring me cookies as welcoming gifts and other surprise goodies when our family is visiting, we have found that Durham is Midwestern enough for my husband (from Ohio), and Southern enough for me, but in a different way. In the Texas of my experience, people must *have* everything; in New York, people must *know* everything. In Durham, we can just *be*—be kind, be thoughtful, be creative, be eccentric, be social or alone, be comfortable in our sweats and sneaks or our cashmere, be from elsewhere and still find a place to fit.

Of course, I have the art and music and culture and intellectual vibes of really, really smart university people, and the fresh market food that my family enjoys when they visit—and my husband has his basketball games. Sitting halfway between Duke and UNC and twenty minutes from friends in Hillsborough, we are in God's country—I love that old Texas cliché, no matter how misplaced. All this, and water too. Water every single day. Right here in Durham.

(I'm thinking of birdnapping a pair of swans. Do you think Mr. Mean Man from Chapel Hill will rat me out?)

CEIL CLEVELAND once ordered a beached Swanboat from Boston Public Gardens for her husband's birthday—until she discovered it was thirty feet long and held twenty people. She is author of a memoir, *Whatever Happened to Jacy Farrow?* as well as books of fiction and nonfiction. She taught creative writing at several universities, most recently at New York University. Founding editor of the award-winning *Columbia Magazine,* she now edits *Eno River Literary Journal.*

Durham Out Loud

The City

(a poem to be read aloud)

GEORGE YAMAZAWA JR.

This war on terrorism is making it dangerous for us to leave this country . . .
But where I'm from
It's dangerous for some to leave their own doorsteps
This violence
Is seeping through the seams of our screen doors
And hijacking the comfort of our own homes . . .
In Durham.

Where the city is economically split into two and each half
Has no idea what the other side is like,
So stereotypes play the role of mutual friends and help them to get to
know each other.
But while stereotypes only inflict a little pain,
The truth is what really hurts.

Gang violence has risen more than fifty percent in the last twenty years.

This conflict reminds me of poetry—
The way the violence turns faces to violets when family members bleed roses
In the City of Bulls . . .
It's no wonder why my boys get caught up in beef
Not everyone can shoot hoops or rip beats
There's limited food and everyone needs to eat
And the only changes we ever see are in the seasons
As grades fall
And hearts turn cold, guns get took out
Triggers spring back
And make barrels hotter than summer cook-outs but don't get this mixed with
no picnic
'Cause this is no walk in the park,
You see this is more like passing through an army base
Where soldiers train year-round for a war against themselves
But there are no medals of honor,
These teens would rather squeeze metal for honor and die clutching their flags
While bleeding their true colors
But, I feel sorry for the mothers.
Who have babies who have babies and it's crazy
We're becoming afraid of our own children in a world that's growing up too fast,
But there must be an answer . . .
Or a cure . . .
Somewhere,

In the City of Medicine
Where it's easier to buy guns and drugs instead of healthcare
So the streets become their hospitals

These OGs play doctor while these kids have nothing but patience
Live ill lives and get sick criminal records

These symptoms are much more severe than the common cold
But just as easy to spread,
It's contagious . . . like the team spirit

Found in the City of Blue Devils . . .
Where UNC ain't the biggest rivalry
It's like Duke and State shoot it out every night but there aren't any
scoreboards,
Just death counts
Red and blue bandana printed uniforms,
Last second shots,
And sharpshooters on both teams . . .
Although I'm not affiliated with either side, I feel like a fan
Just watching the action happen.
But this game is taking too long—it's too bad there are no ties in basketball
Because overtime,
Nobody wins . . . so what are these suicides for?
We are killing ourselves
I wish I could turn our OGs into CEOs,
Hustlers into mathematicians,
And gangbangers into painters . . .
So hopefully they could put these colors to better use.
And the pigs?
I'd turn them into police officers respected by everybody
But the snakes—I'd make them doctors
So they can change their poisons into medicines
That would heal the crack addicts

Who would become Saints
After living in a life of hell

Where grouches count stacks from selling big birds
But this is far from Sesame Street,
More like Fayetteville St.,
Hoover St.,
South St.,
The Southside,
The West End and
East Durham,
But on Massey Chapel Rd. . . .
Far away from all the noise in the city
I can still hear the orchestra that Durham is conducting,
And it just doesn't sound right.
So please . . . I'm begging you . . .
Stop the violin-ce.

GEORGE YAMAZAWA JR. was born and raised in Durham and is considered one of the top young spoken word artists in the country. Twenty-one years old, he is an Individual World Poetry Slam Finalist, National Poetry Slam Finalist, and two-time Southern Fried Champion. He is a founding member of the Sacrificial Poets, three-time member of the Bull City Slam Team, and has performed in venues across the United States, including at the Sundance Film Festival. He loves fried chicken and hates sushi.

One Square Mile

A Durham Anthem

[Editor's note: To hear Rebecca sing "One Square Mile: A Durham Anthem" in all its musical glory, you can download an MP3 at www.reverbnation.com/rebeccanewton.]

Below 3 rivers in '81
Through Durham Station the trains would run
From north to south, from east to west
So a county was formed that tobacco loved best.

'Twas a black man's cure and a white man's lust
That gave us the Bright Leaf and money from dust
2000 a day, each woman would roll
Soon the city was famous, in Egypt and all.

Tobacco was king for a century or more
Now it's medicine, baseball, and fancy food stores
The young people bring in the new and diverse
While old-timers pine, some mumble — some curse.

Lived most of my life within one square mile
Got 4 generations and 3 young smiles
When it comes full circle, I'll take my rest
In this old Bull City, that gave me my best.

It was always the music that spoke to me
Our common thread of creativity
I reckon that's why I never stayed gone
I've had a good life here, generous and long.

Lived most of my life within one square mile
Got 4 generations and 3 young smiles
When it comes full circle, I'll take my rest
In this old Bull City, that gave me my best.

And old Proctor plays his fiddle on the Bull City streets
Nearly 40 years now, still steady on his feet
Telling stories in song of this fine old town
Bull Durham, our city, world renown.

Lived most of my life within one square mile
Got 4 generations and 3 young smiles
When it comes full circle, I'll take my rest
In this old Bull City, that gave me my best
I thank this Bull City, it gave me my best.

REBECCA NEWTON found herself in Durham at age thirteen. Despite several attempts to flee, she remains a mile away from where her Durham life began in 1969. She has been a Durham musician since 1975, writing music for plays and for Rebecca & the Hi-Tones, her band of thirty years. Her day job is Chief Community & Safety Officer for Mind Candy, a kids digital entertainment company.

About the Cover

The cover illustration for *27 Views of Durham* is the work of Chapel Hill novelist and artist Daniel Wallace. His illustrations have appeared in many publications, including the *Los Angeles Times*, *Italian Vanity Fair*, and *Our State Magazine*. He also illustrated the book covers of *27 Views of Hillsborough*, *27 Views of Chapel Hill*, and *27 Views of Asheville*, all published by Eno Publishers.

Award-winning Books from Eno Publishers

27 Views of Asheville
A Southern Mountain Town in Prose & Poetry
INTRODUCTION BY ROB NEUFELD
$15.95/210 pages

27 Views of Chapel Hill
A Southern Town in Prose & Poetry
INTRODUCTION BY DANIEL WALLACE
$16.50/240 pages
Bronze IPPY Book Award, Best Regional Nonfiction
Bronze Foreword Book of the Year, Best Anthology

27 Views of Hillsborough
A Southern Town in Prose & Poetry
INTRODUCTION BY MICHAEL MALONE
$15.95/216 pages
Gold IPPY Book Award, Best Anthology
Gold Eric Hoffer Book Award, Culture

Chapel Hill in Plain Sight
Notes from the Other Side of the Tracks
DAPHNE ATHAS
$16.95/246 pages

Undaunted Heart
The True Story of a Southern Belle & a Yankee General
SUZY BARILE
$16.95/238 pages
Silver IPPY Book Award, Best Regional Nonfiction

Brook Trout & the Writing Life
The Intermingling of Fishing & Writing in a Novelist's Life
CRAIG NOVA
$15.95 / 152 pages

Rain Gardening in the South
Ecologically Designed Gardens for Drought,
Deluge & Everything in Between
HELEN KRAUS & ANNE SPAFFORD
$19.95 / 144 pages
Gold Book Award, Garden Writers Association
Silver Book Award, Garden Writers Association
Silver Benjamin Franklin Book Award
Honorable Mention, Eric Hoffer Book Award

Eno's books are available at your local bookshop,
and from www.enopublishers.org